Name________________________________

Words With a

p a r k a r b r k
q c a f r c a a j
s c r f n a r r a
s c a r f r n n r
j c a r f t r t y
x y a r n a r n a
y a r s t a r a r

park

cart

scarf

jar

car

star

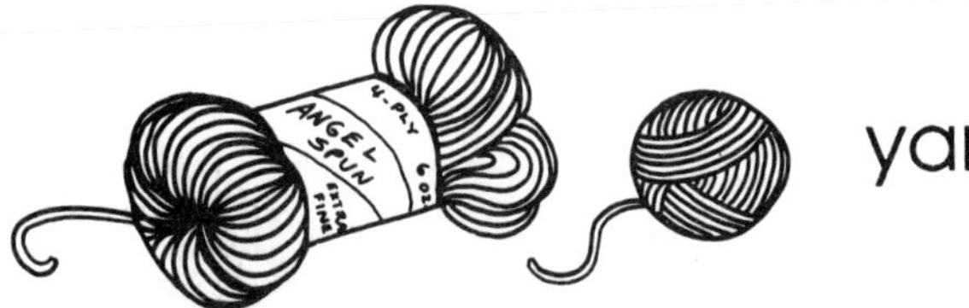
ANGEL
SPUN
4-PLY

yarn

barn

Name____

Words With *ar*

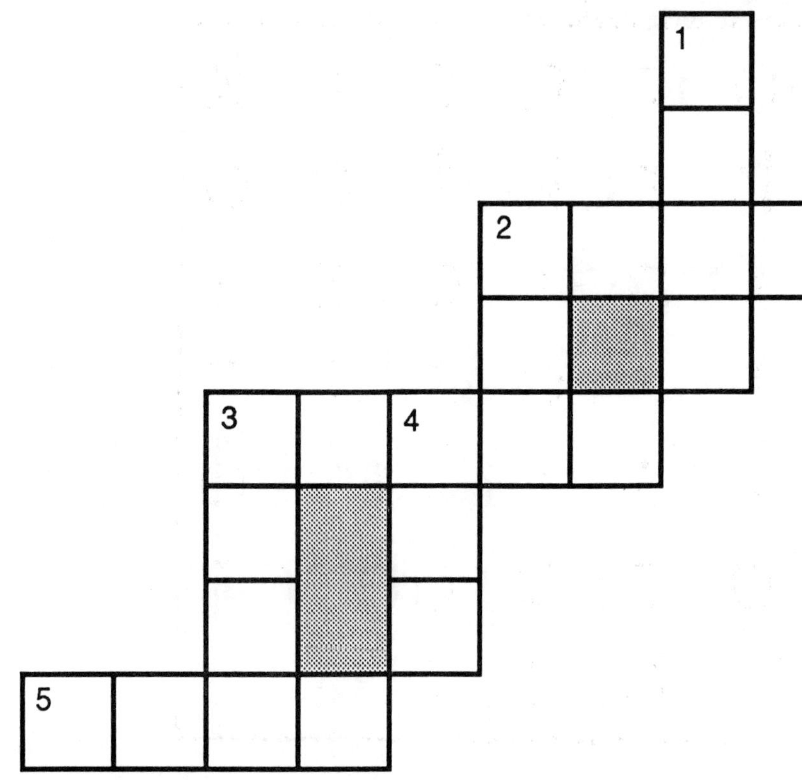

Word Box
star
arm
car
cart
scarf
card
barn

Across

2. 

HAPPY EASTER
May your day be...

3. 

5. 

Down

1. 

2. 

3. 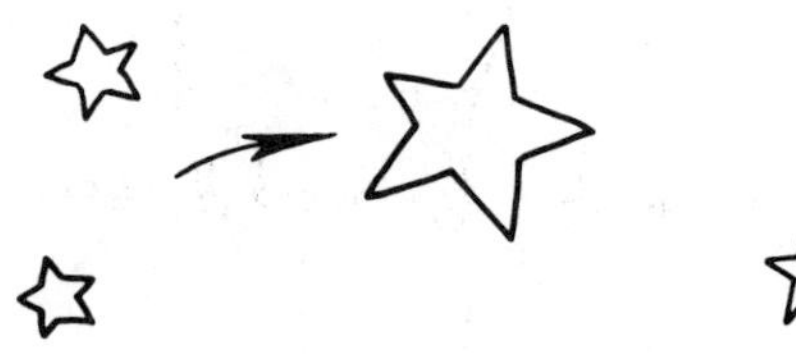

4. 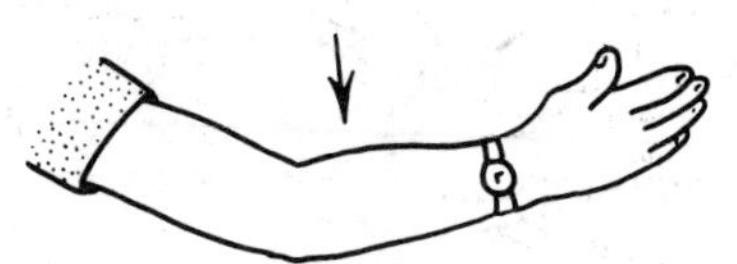

Words With *or*

c	o	z	c	o	r	n	s	r	k
o	s	t	r	k	r	k	t	c	o
r	e	h	o	r	n	r	o	z	s
k	c	h	q	r	s	e	r	r	t
s	e	r	e	r	s	r	k	c	o
r	k	k	t	o	r	c	h	h	r
f	o	r	k	z	h	o	r	s	e

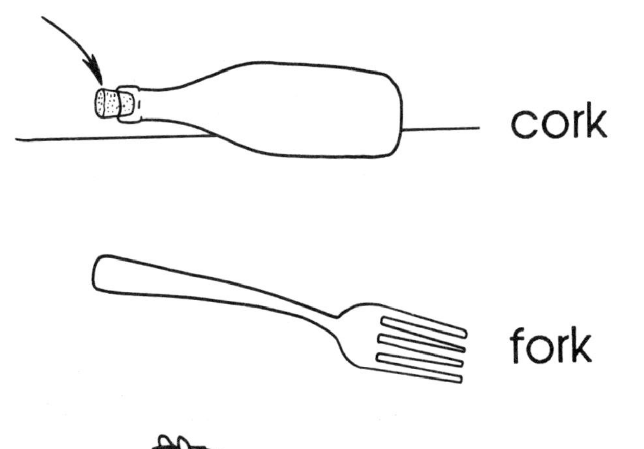

cork

fork

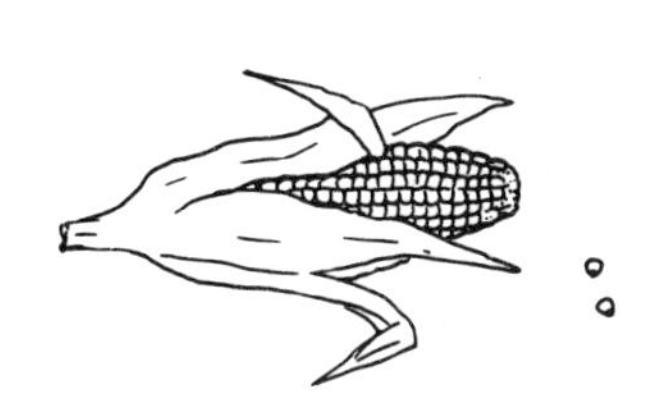

corn

horn

horse

SALE
PEACHES 59¢
PLUMS
49¢ /pound
ENTER
EXIT
SANTA

store

stork

torch

Name________________________________ Special vowels

Words With *or*

1
2
3
4
5
6
7

Word Box
horn
horse
fork
stork
torch
corn
store
cork

Across

2. 

3.

6. 

7. 

Down

1. 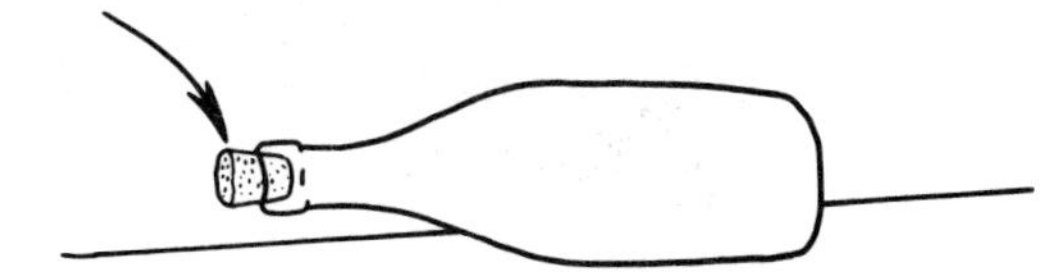

2. 

SALE
PEACHES 59¢
PLUMS
49¢ /pound
ENTER
EXIT
SANTA

4. 

5. 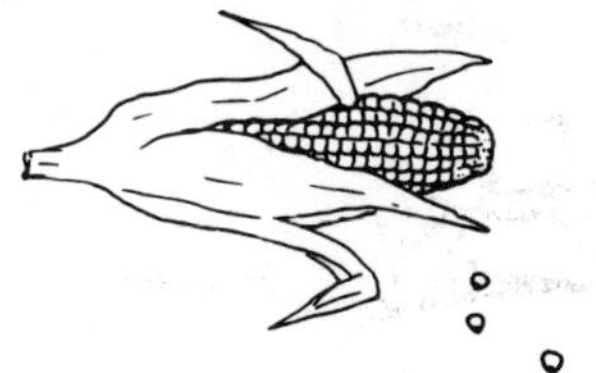

Name____

Words With *er* and *ir*

s	k	s	k	i	r	t	r	g
f	r	u	l	e	r	q	u	i
e	b	i	r	r	r	u	l	r
r	s	l	e	t	t	e	r	l
n	b	i	r	d	t	t	e	r
f	s	q	u	i	r	r	e	l
e	s	h	i	r	t	s	h	i

bird

girl

fern

skirt

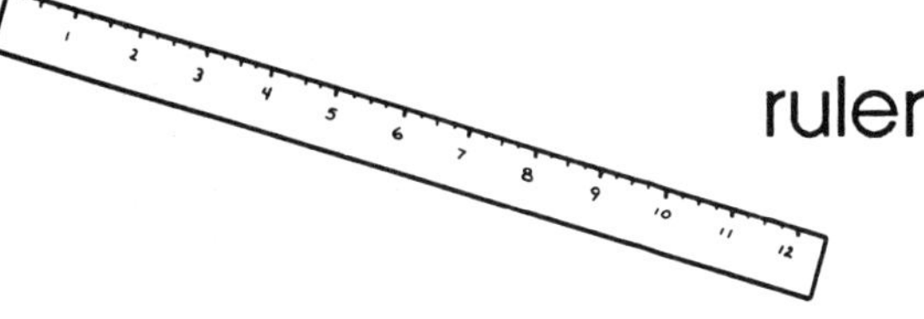
1
2
3
4
5
6
7
8
9
10
11
12

ruler

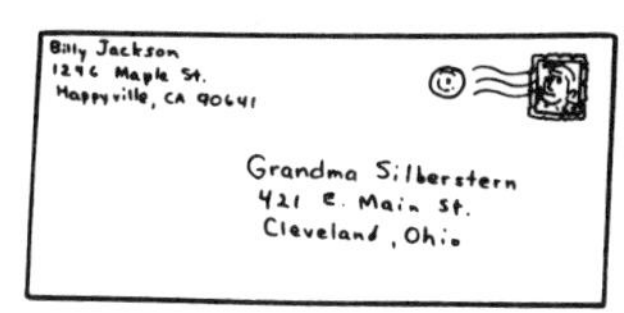
Billy Jackson
1296 Maple St.
Happyville, CA 90641
Grandma Silberstern
421 E. Main St.
Cleveland, Ohio

letter

squirrel

shirt

Name______________________________ Special vowels

Words With *er* and *ir*

1
2
3
4
5
6

Word Box

fern
girl
letter
ruler
shirt
skirt
squirrel

Across

1. 

4. 

5. 

6. 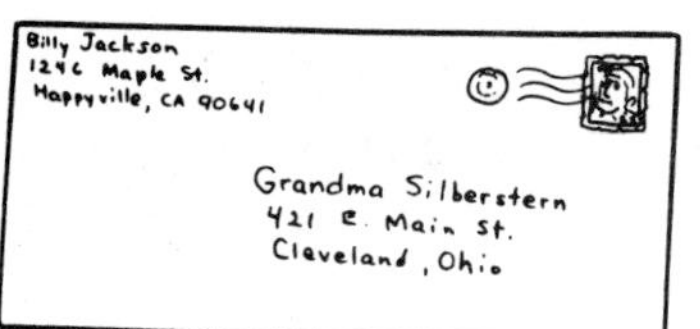

Billy Jackson
1246 Maple St.
Happyville, CA 90641
Grandma Silberstern
421 E. Main St.
Cleveland, Ohio

Down

1. 

2. 

3. 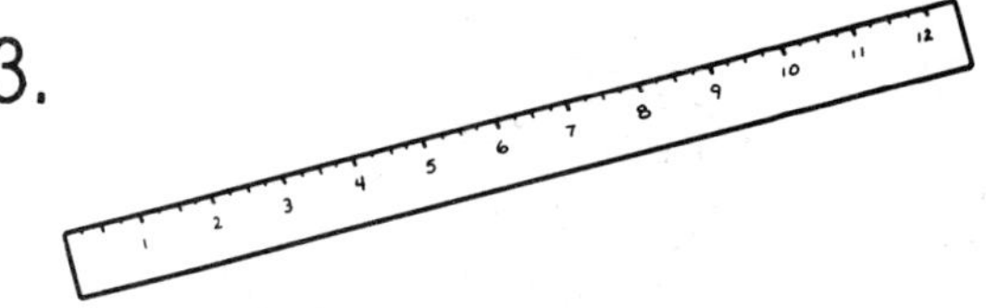

Name ____________________

Words with *ir* and *ur*

1
2
3
4
5
6

Word Box
church
curl
nurse
purse
skirt
squirrel
turkey
turtle

Across

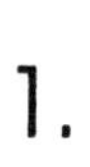

1. 

2. 

5. 

6. 

Down

1. 

2. 

3. 

4. 

Name____

Words With *ea* and *ey*

m	o	n	k	e	y	k	e	b	t
h	s	w	e	a	t	e	r	r	h
h	s	w	k	e	y	n	k	e	r
e	y	n	k	m	n	e	y	a	e
a	f	e	a	t	h	e	r	d	a
d	c	h	i	m	n	e	y	y	d

monkey

sweater

head

key

feather

chimney

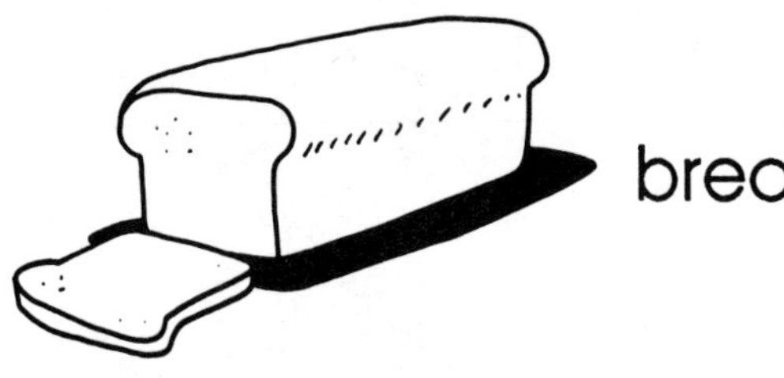

bread

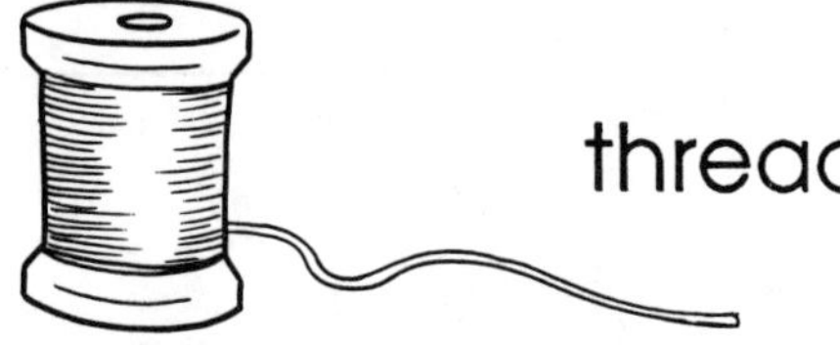

thread

Name____ Special vowels

Words With *ea* and *ey*

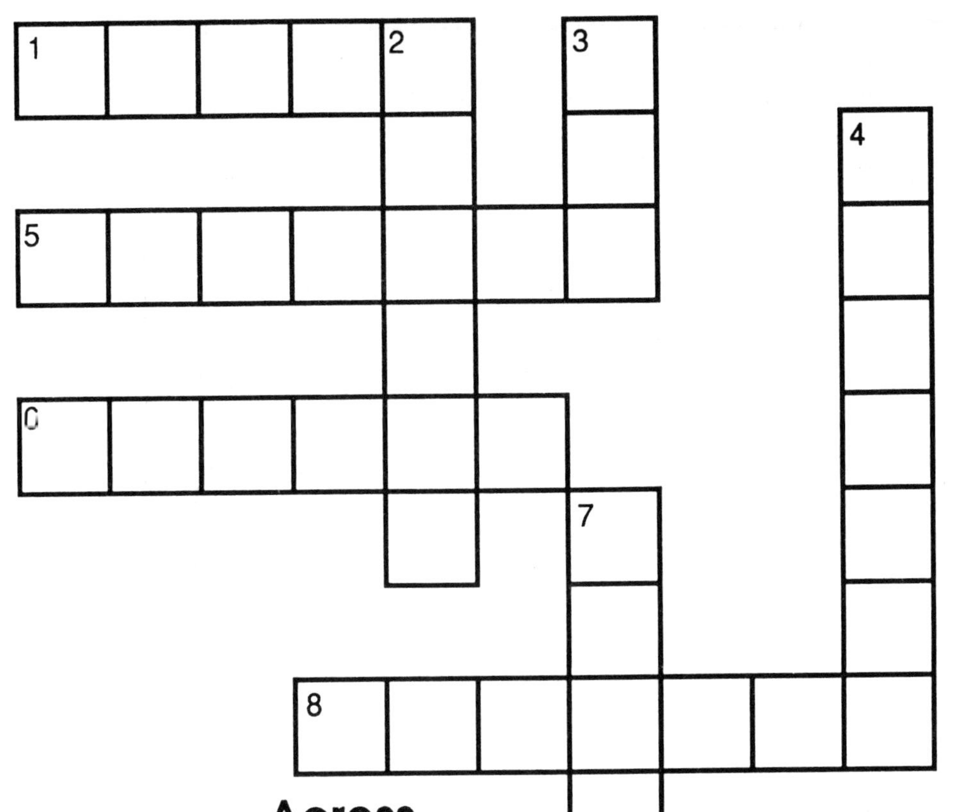

1
2
3
4
5
6
7
8

Word Box
bread
chimney
donkey
feather
head
key
monkey
sweater

Across

1. 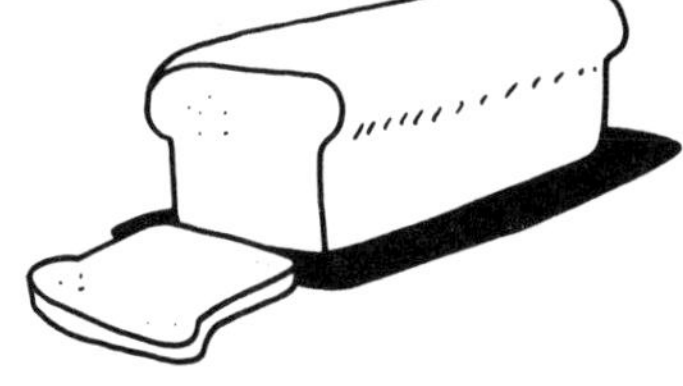

5. 

6. 

8. 

Down

2. 

3. 

4. 

7. 

Name____ Special vowels

Words With *ew* and *ow*

w	w	i	n	d	o	w	j	s
i	w	m	n	d	l	l	s	c
b	p	i	l	l	o	w	t	r
o	j	e	s	n	s	n	e	e
w	j	e	w	e	l	r	w	w
l	s	c	r	o	w	p	i	l
s	n	o	w	m	a	n	j	e

jewel

crow

window

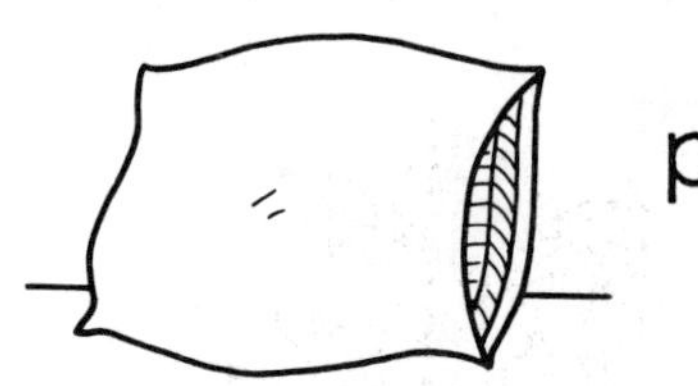

pillow

bowl

snowman

stew

screw

Name____

Words with *ew* and *ow*

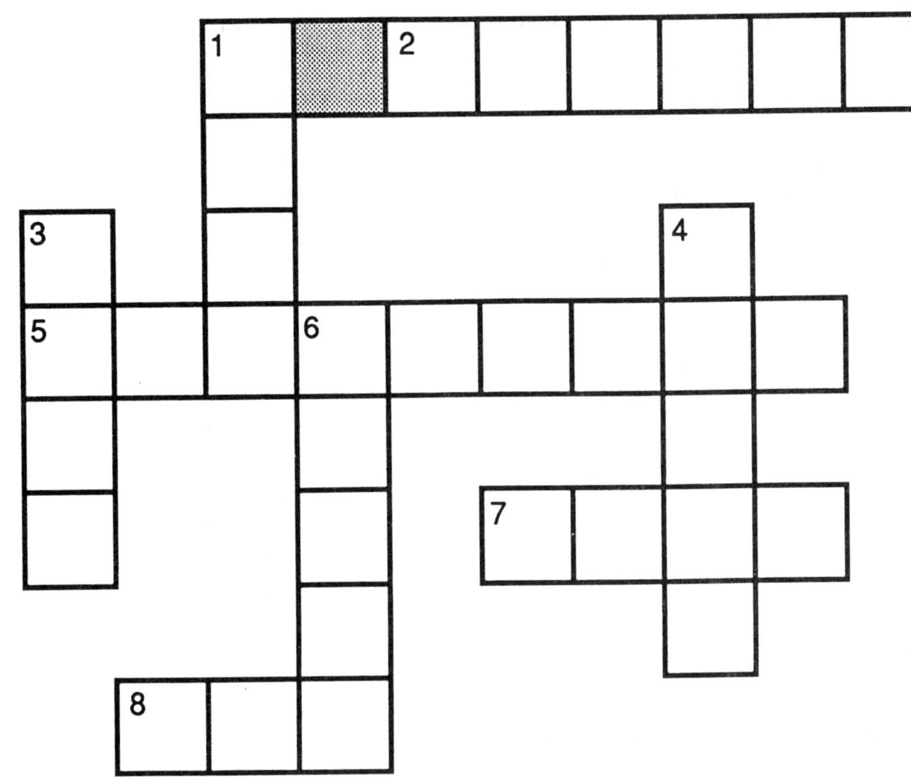

Word Box
bow
crow
jewel
newspaper
pillow
screw
snow
stew

Down

2. 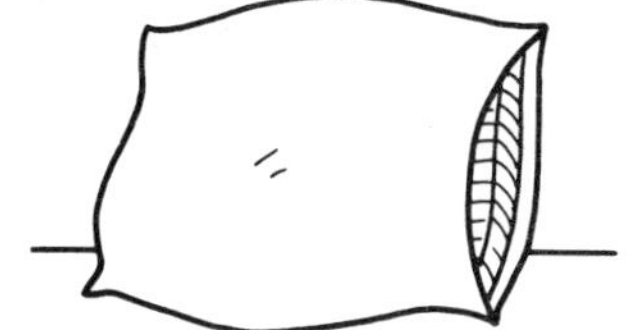

1. 

5. 
DAILY NEWS

3. 

7. 

4. 

8. 

6. 

Name____

Words With *ow*

c	l	c	l	o	w	n	w	n
r	g	o	w	n	l	w	n	e
o	f	l	n	t	o	w	e	l
w	w	o	w	l	q	q	x	w
d	w	n	c	r	o	w	n	n
d	f	l	o	w	e	r	e	l

clown

gown

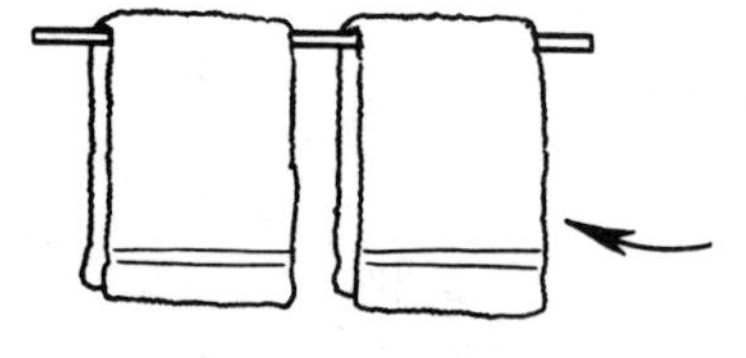
towel

flower

owl

crown

crowd

Name____

Words With *ou*

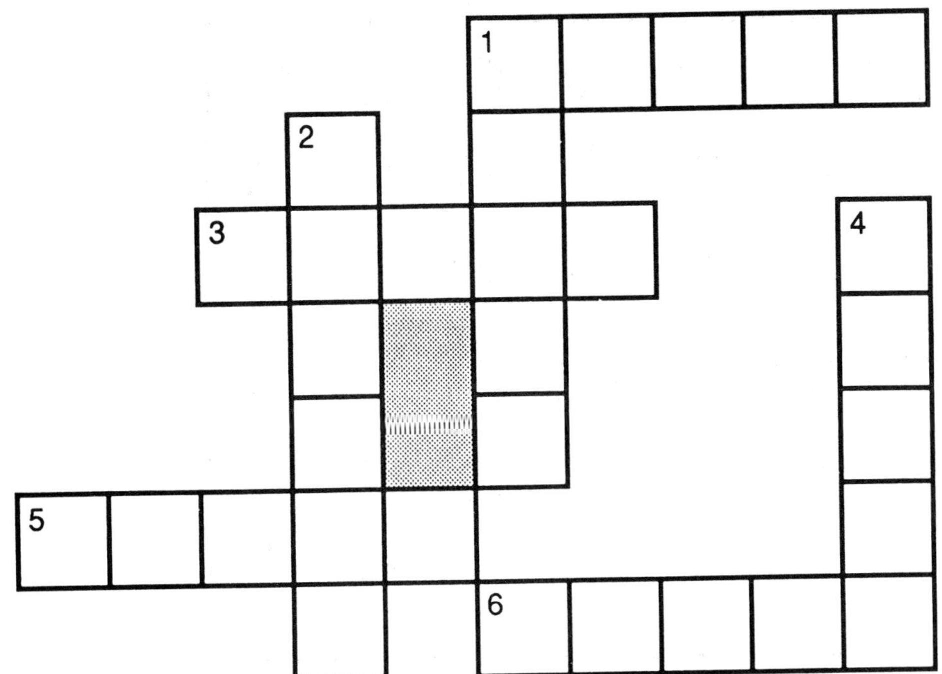
1
2
3
4
5
6

Word Box
blouse
cloud
hound
house
mouse
mouth
pouch

Across

1. 

3. 

5. 

6. 

Down

1. 

2. 

4. 

Name____ Special vowels

Words With *oo*

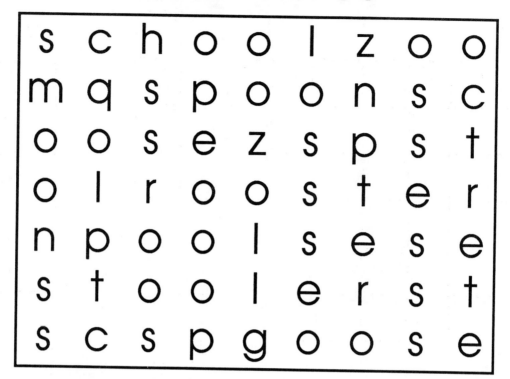

s	c	h	o	o	l	z	o	o
m	q	s	p	o	o	n	s	c
o	o	s	e	z	s	p	s	t
o	l	r	o	o	s	t	e	r
n	p	o	o	l	s	e	s	e
s	t	o	o	l	e	r	s	t
s	c	s	p	g	o	o	s	e

school

spoon

rooster

pool

moon

goose

zoo

stool

Name____

Words With *oo*

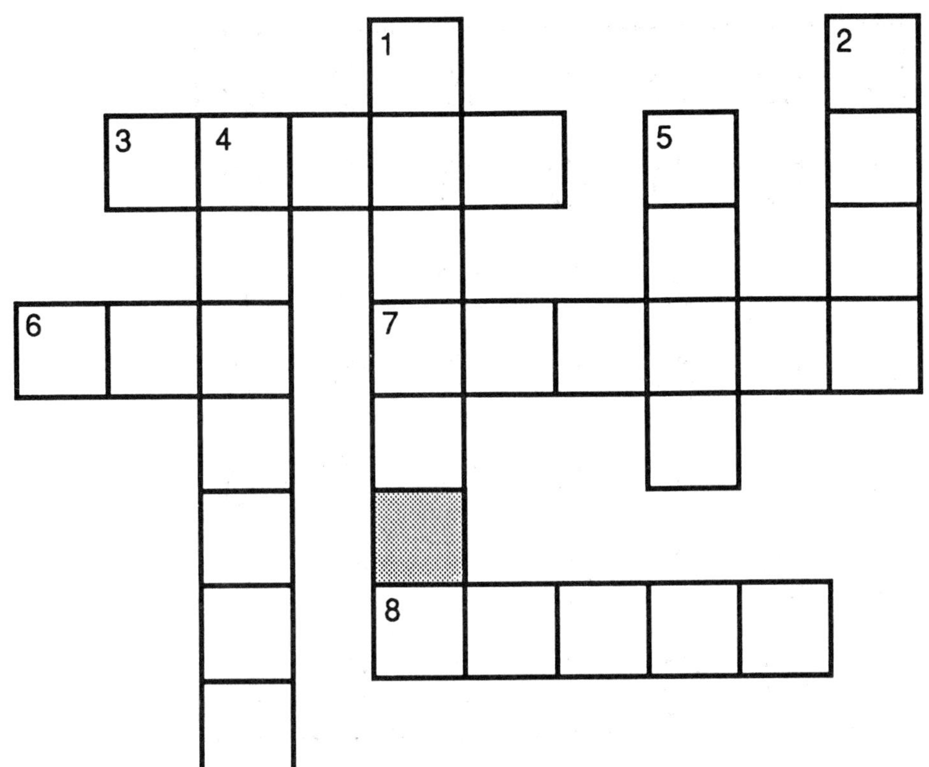
1
2
3
4
5
6
7
8

Word Box
broom
moon
pool
rooster
school
tooth
zoo
goose

Across

3. 

6.

7. 

8. 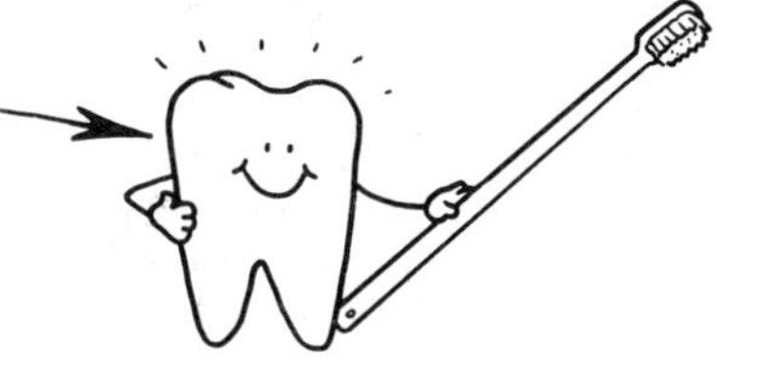

Down

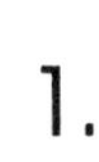
1. 

2. 

4. 

5.  

Name____

Words With *oi* and *oy*

n	o	i	s	e	b	o	y	t
s	p	o	i	n	t	i	l	o
e	b	q	o	y	i	o	o	y
p	c	o	i	n	z	i	i	l
n	c	o	z	s	e	l	e	n
t	x	s	o	i	l	o	y	t
c	o	i	l	q	c	o	i	u

coil

oil

toy

point

soil

boy

coin

noise

Name____

Words With *oi* and *oy*

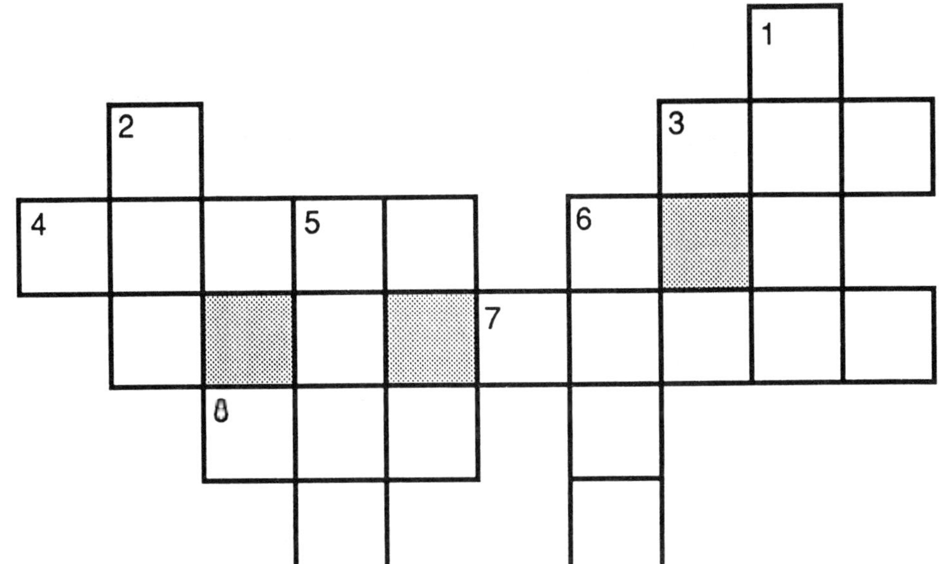
1
2
3
4
5
6
7
8

Word Box
- boy
- coil
- coin
- noise
- point
- oil
- soil
- toy

Across

3. 

4. 

7. 

8. 

Down

1. 

2. 

5. 

6. 

Name____________________

Words With *oo* and *oy*

b	o	o	k	o	v	o	o	k
o	d	b	k	o	c	o	o	k
q	h	o	o	d	w	o	d	h
x	o	o	o	b	k	b	x	o
w	o	o	d	c	k	o	o	o
w	o	m	t	o	y	y	y	k
f	o	o	t	c	o	q	o	t

wood

boy

toy

book

hood

S
P

cook

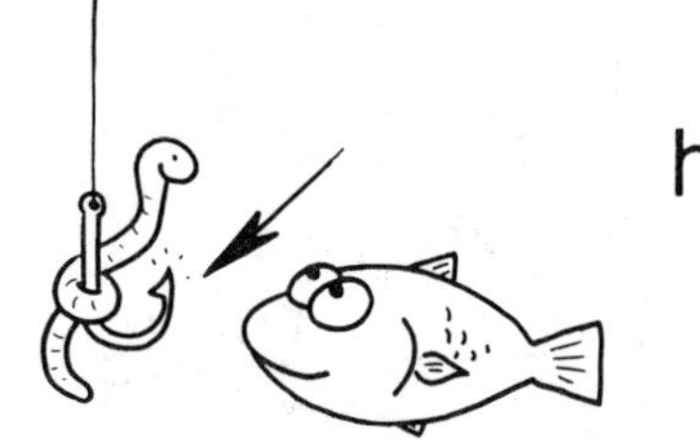

hook

foot

Name________________________________

Words With *oo* and *oy*

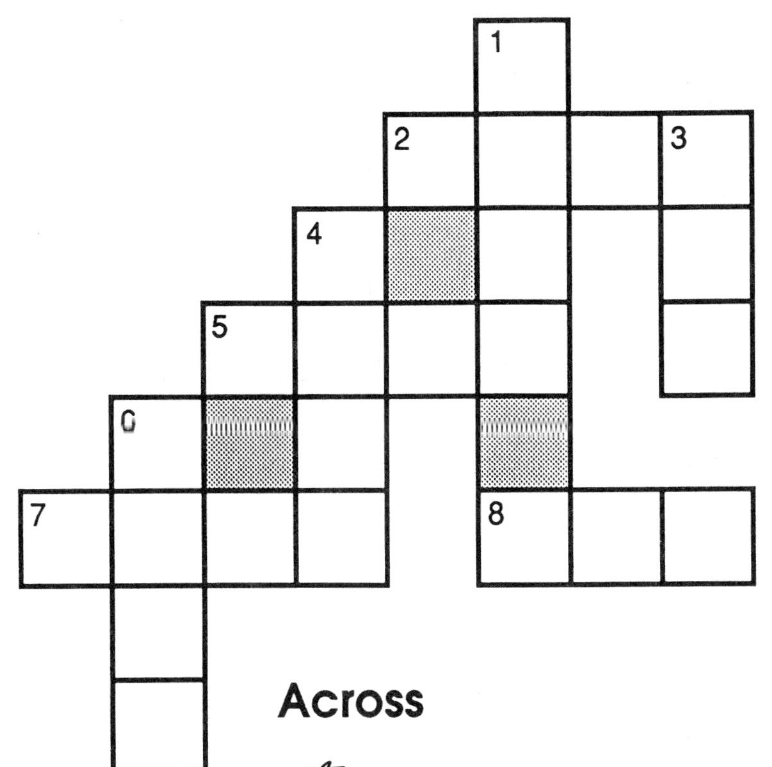
1
2
3
4
5
6
7
8

Word Box
- boy
- book
- cook
- foot
- hood
- hook
- toy
- wood

Across

2. 

5. 

7. 

8. 

Down

1. 

3. 

4. 

6. 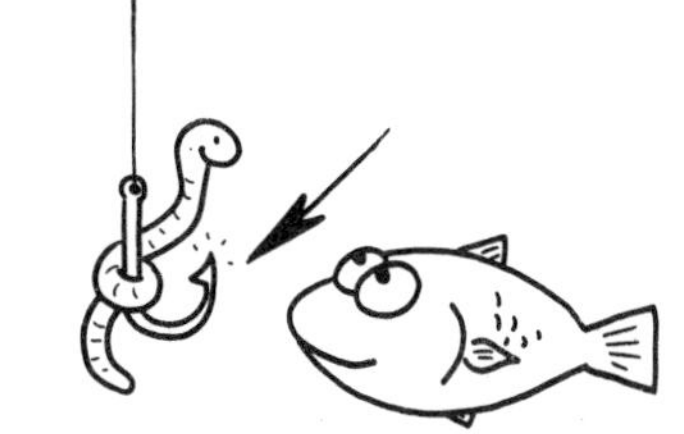

Name____

Words With *aw* and *au*

s	t	r	a	w	t	r	A	a
A	u	g	u	s	t	h	u	u
c	l	d	r	a	w	a	u	t
p	a	w	w	k	r	w	t	u
y	a	w	n	r	w	k	r	m
c	l	a	w	f	w	n	w	n
s	a	w	f	a	w	n	w	n

yawn

hawk

AUGUST

August

claw

draw

straw

fawn

autumn

paw

saw

Name ____

A Happy Thought:

chomp
chomp
YUMMY

W ___ ___ ___ h   ___ ___ ___   f ___ ___   ___ h ___
(W 3 1 4 h   8 6 1   f 8 7   1 h 2)

___ ___ ___ k ___ ___   m ___ n s ___ ___ ___ ! !
(4 8 8 k 5 2   m 8 n s 1 2 7 ! !)

1.	2.	3.	4.

ha ___	b ___ d	c ___ p	___ at
5.	**6.**	**7.**	**8.**
			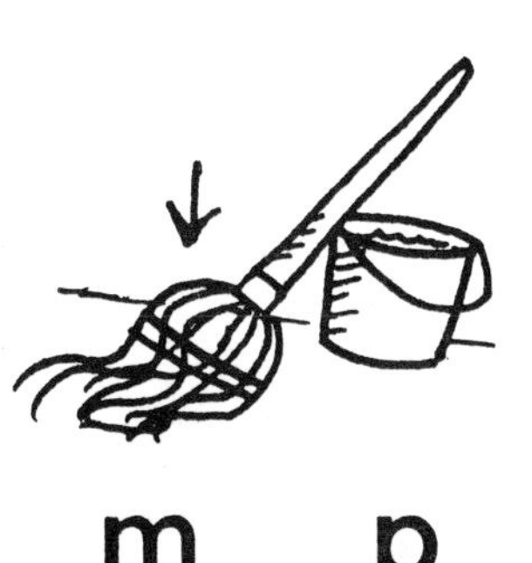
p ___ n	s ___ n	___ at	m ___ p

Name ______________________________

A Riddle:

Why do elephants have flat feet?

Aha!

f r _3_ _7_   j _8_ _7_ _2_ _6_ n g   _3_ _8_ _5_

_3_ f   _2_ _1_ l _7_   _5_ r _4_ _4_ s

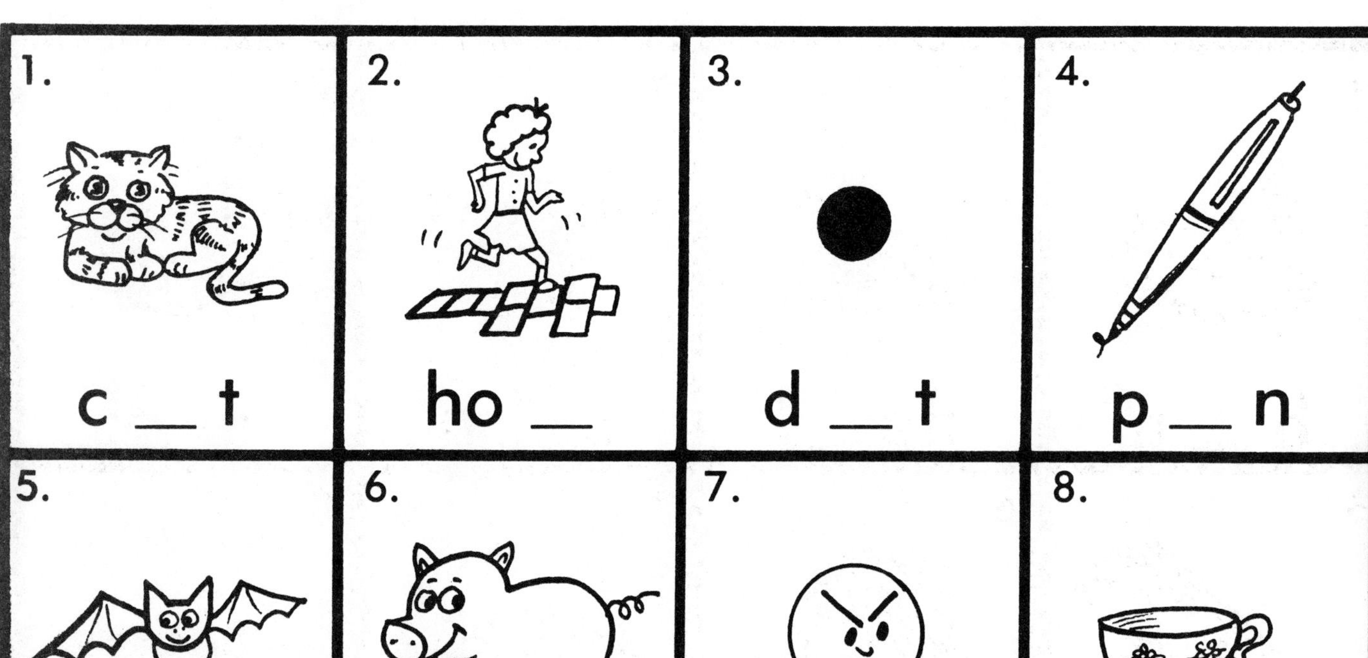
1.
c __ t
2.
ho __
3.
d __ t
4.
p __ n

5.

ba __

6.

p __ g

7.

__ ad

8.

c __ p

Name ____

Well, I'll eat anywhere!

A Riddle:
At what table do you never sit to eat?

m	__	__	__	__	p	__	__	c	__	__	__	__	n
	5	7	2	6		7	6		3	2	6	8	

__	__	__	__	__
2	3	4	7	1

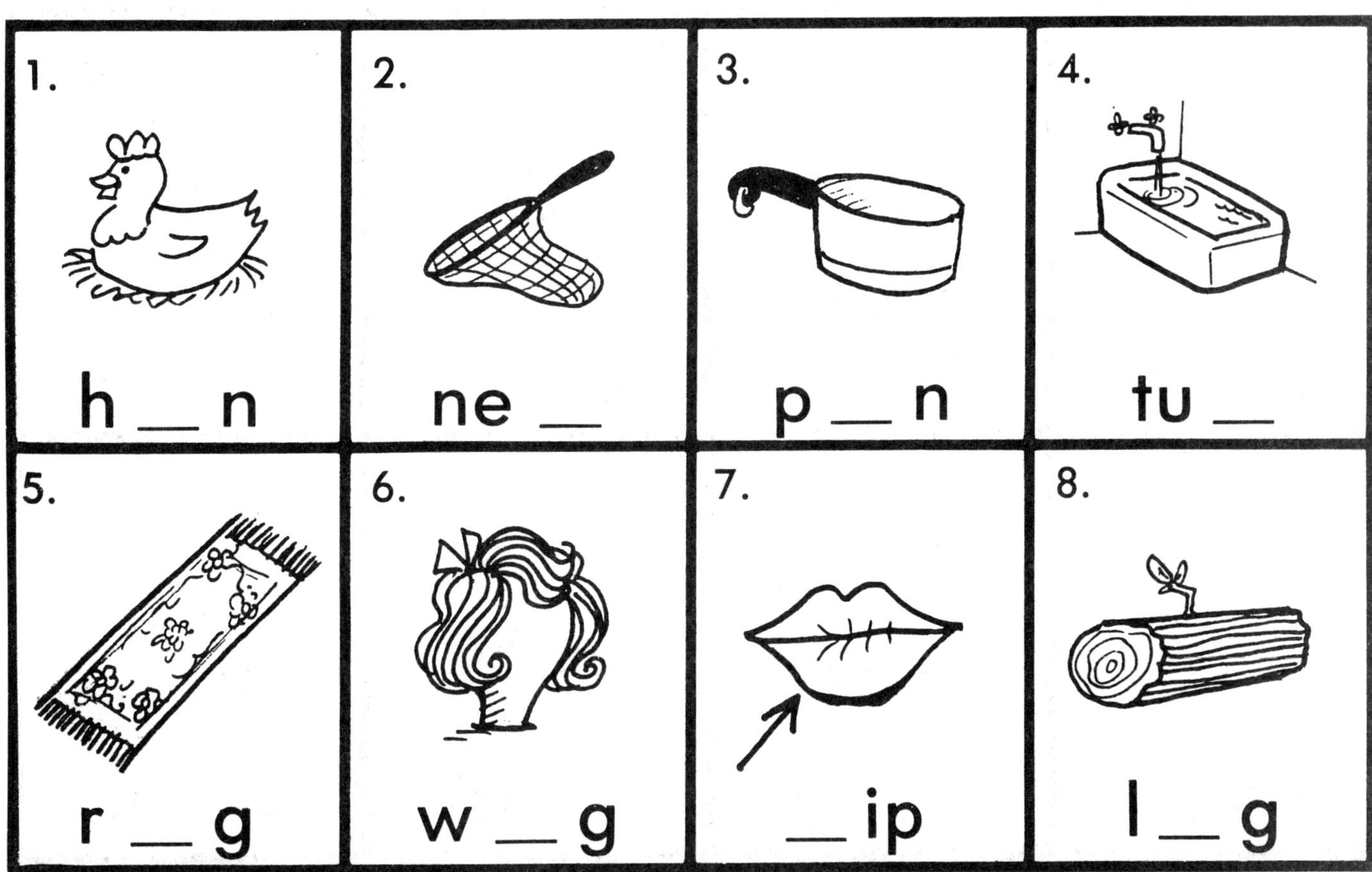

1.

h __ n

2.

ne __

3.

p __ n

4.

tu __

5.

r __ g

6.

w __ g

7.
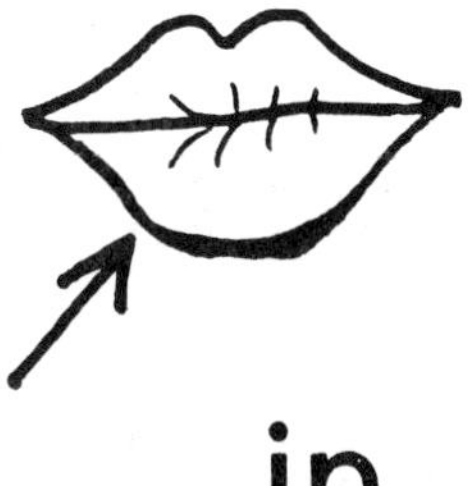
__ ip

8.

l __ g

Name______________________________

A Tongue Twister:

Ho ho
Aha ha!
tee hee

F	__	v	__		__	__	t		__	__	__	__	y
6	8		2		6	4			6	7	1	1	

__	__	__	__	__	w	s		__	__	__	__		__	__	__	__	.
6	2	3	3	5				6	2	2	3		6	8	1	2	

1.

me __

2.

t __ n

3.

__ ock

4.

PEARS IN
c __ n

5.

j __ g

6.

__ an

7.

j __ g

8.

p __ g

Name____

A Riddle:
How many sides does a coconut have?

__	w	__	-	__	__	s	__	__	__		__	__	__
6		1		7	2		7	8	5		4	2	8

__	__	__	s	__	__	__
1	3	6		7	8	5

1. 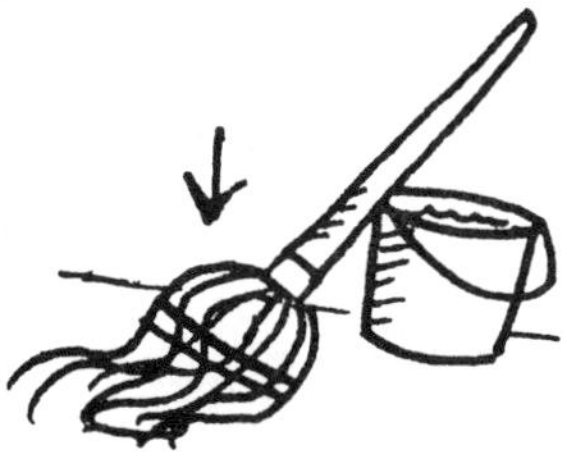 m __ p	2.  __ est	3.  b __ g	4.  h __ m
5.  j __ t	6.  ve __	7.  b __ b	8.  da __

Name ________________________________

A Happy Thought:

sigh
I wouldn't know.

___ ___ ___ ___ h ___ ___ ___   c ___ ___   b ___
7 3 5 2 · 6 8 2   · 3 8   · 1

___ ___ t s   ___ f   f ___ ___ .
7 4 · ·   4 ·   · 5 8

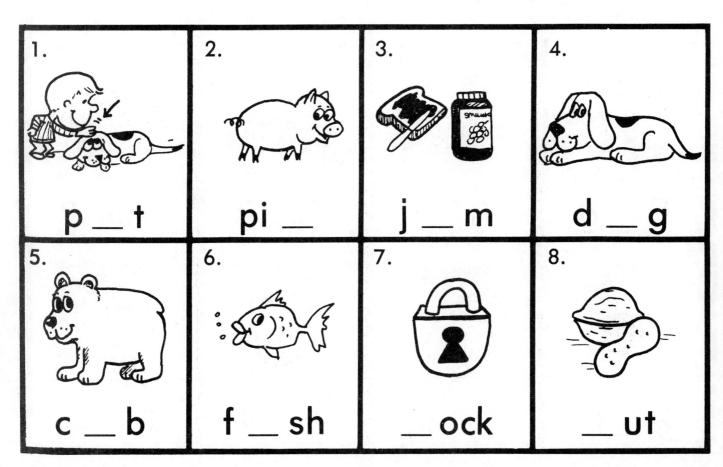

1.

p __ t

2.

pi __

3.

j __ m

4.

d __ g

5.

c __ b

6.

f __ sh

7.

__ ock

8.

__ ut

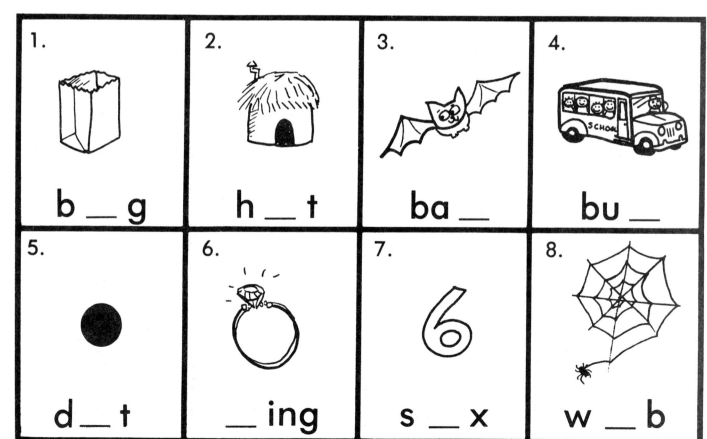

Name____________________

A Riddle:

Why is the word lilies like a face?

Hmm.

b ___ c ___ ___ ___ ___ ___ h ___ ___ ___ ___ ___ ___
8, 1 2 4 8, 3, 8 6 8, 1 6 8

___ w ___ ___ ' ___ ___ n ___ ___
3, 5, 7, 4, 7, 7 3

1.  b __ g	2.  h __ t	3.  ba __	4.  bu __
5.  d __ t	6.  __ ing	7.  s __ x	8.  w __ b

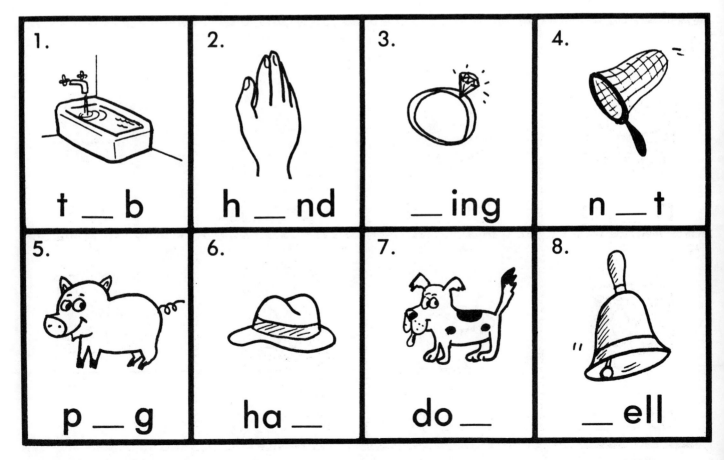

Name ______________________________

For me?

A Tongue Twister:

_   _ _ _   _ _ _ y   _ _ _ _ y
2   8 5 7   8 2 8   8 1 7 7

w _ _ h   _ _ _ _ _ _   _ _ _ _ y
5 6   3 1 8 8 4 3   8 1 7 7

_ _ m p _ _ s
8 1   4 3

1. 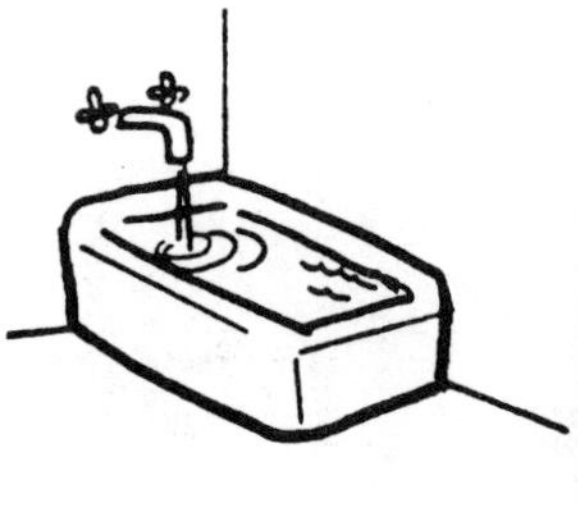 t _ b	2. 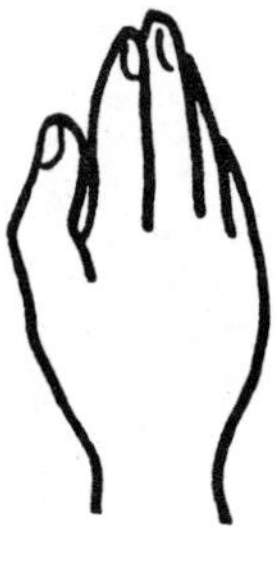 h _ nd	3.  _ ing	4.  n _ t
5.  p _ g	6.  ha _	7.  do _	8.  _ ell

Name ______________________________

A Riddle:

What was the elephant doing on Route 495?

There he is!

___	b	___	___	___		___	h	r	___	___		___	___	l	___	s
8		6	1	4		4			2	2		5	3		2	

___	___		h	___	___	r
8	7			6	1	

1.	2.	3.	4.

h __ g	b __ ll	p __ n	__ en
5.	**6.**	**7.**	**8.**
			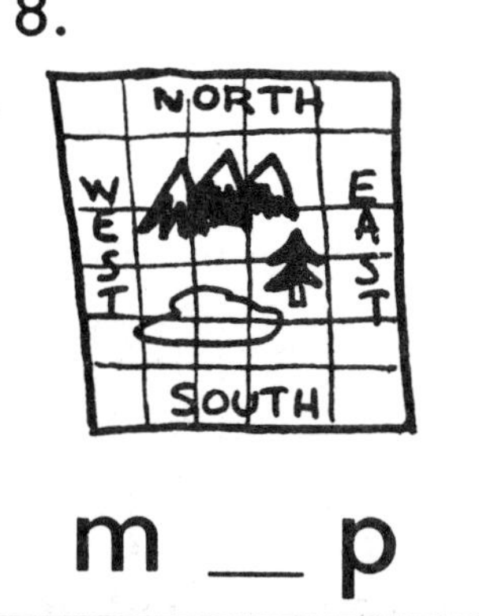 NORTH WEST EAST SOUTH
dru __	t __ p	ki __ g	m __ p

Name ____

A Riddle:

What happens when an owl has a sore throat?

__ __   __ __ __ s n ' __   __ __ v __

7 2   5 8 2 s n ' 3   4 1 v 2

__   __ __ __ __ .

6   7 8 8 3 .

1. 
   k __ ng
2. 
   w __ ll
3. 
   ca __
4. 
   ru __
5. 
   sa __
6. 
   fl __ g
7. 
   __ op
8. 
   d __ ll

Name ____

Boo!

A Riddle:

What do you do with a blue monster?

__ __ __ __ __ __ __ __ __ __
5 3 1 1 8 3 6 2 4 7

1.	2.	3.	4.
 dr __ ss	 __ en	 __ am	 s __ n
5.	**6.**	**7.**	**8.**
 __ at	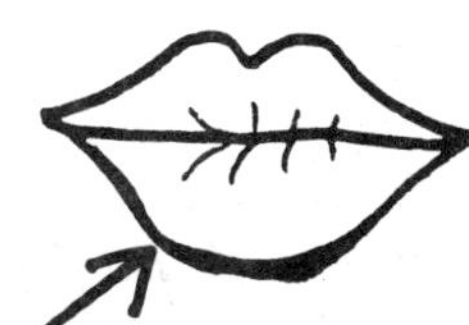 l __ p	 __ ig	 __ at

Name_______________________________

A Riddle:

What has nails

but no hammer?

I have
both.

y __ __ __   __ __ __ __ __ __ s
4 1 6   2 3 5 8 7 6

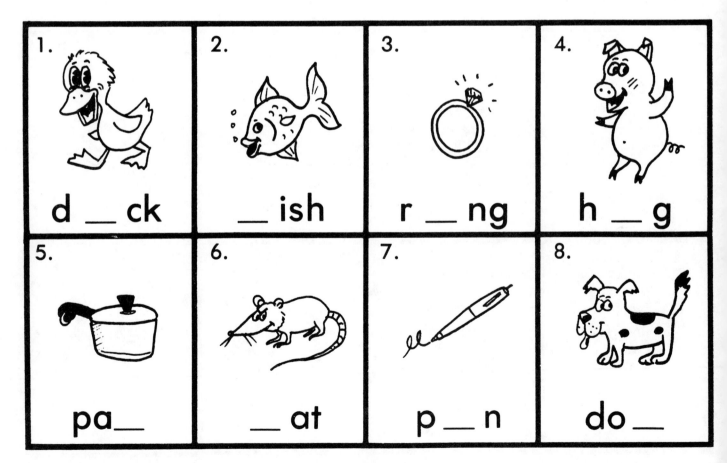

1. d __ ck	2. __ ish	3. r __ ng	4. h __ g
5. pa__	6. __ at	7. p __ n	8. do __

Name ______________________________

A Riddle:

Why does a flamingo stand on one leg?

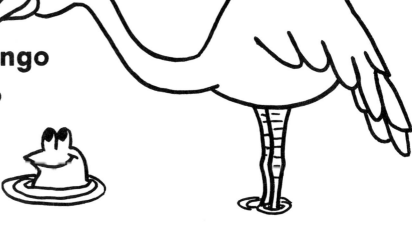

_ _   _ _   c _ _   _ _ _ _   _ _ _
8 2   5 3   1 6   7 3 8 4   4 5 3

_ _ _ _ _   _ _ _
2 4 5 3 7   2 6 3

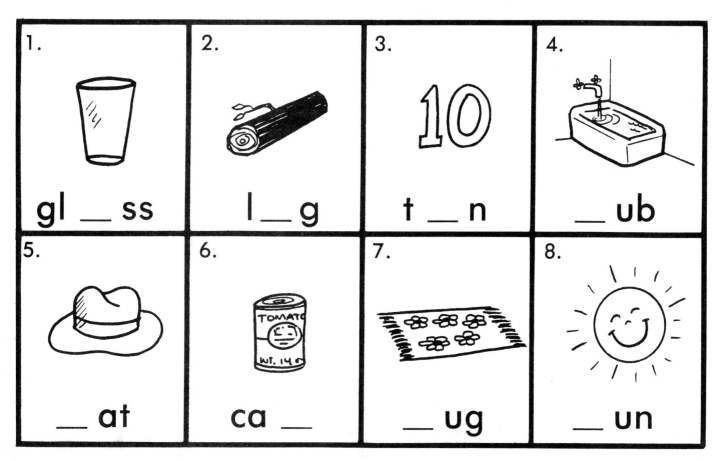

1.  gl __ ss	2.  l __ g	3.  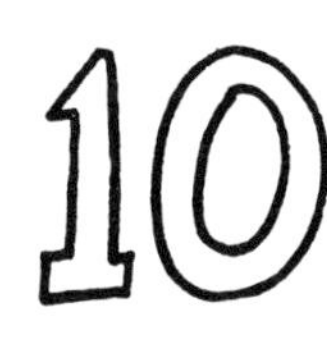 t __ n	4.  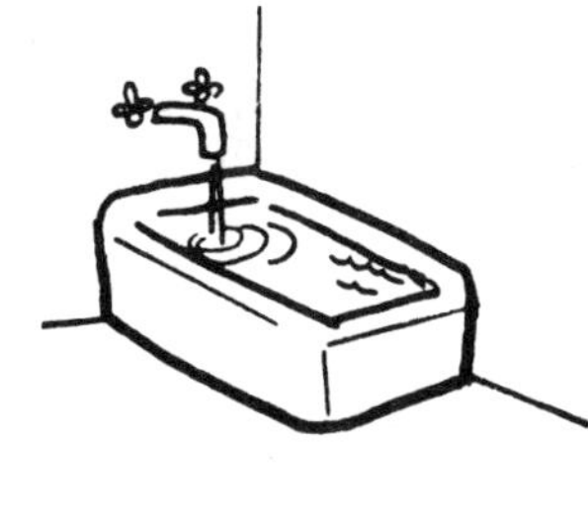 __ ub
5.  __ at	6.  ca __	7.  __ ug	8.  __ un

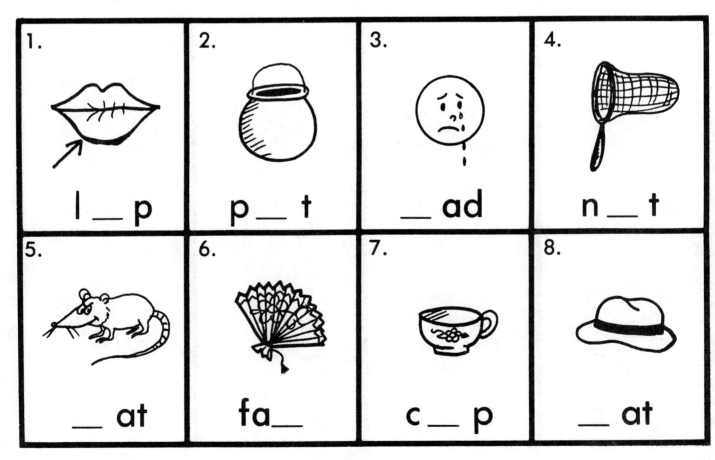

Name________________________________

A Riddle:

What is green and white with red legs and blue teeth?

T ___ ___ ___ ___   ___ ___   ___ ___ ___   ___ ___
   8 4 5 4   1 3   2 6 4   2 6

y ___ ___ ___   ___ ___ ___ ___   l   d ___ ___ .
   2 7 5   3 8 2 7   4 5

1. 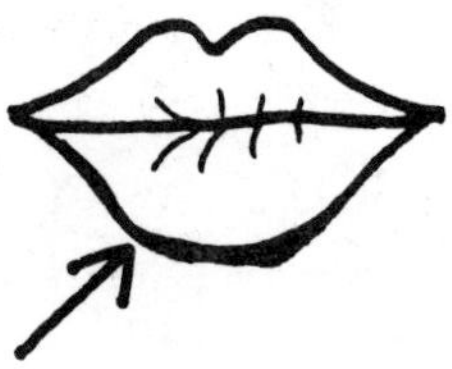 l __ p	2.  p __ t	3.  __ ad	4.  n __ t
5.  __ at	6.  fa__	7.  c __ p	8.  __ at

Name ______________________________

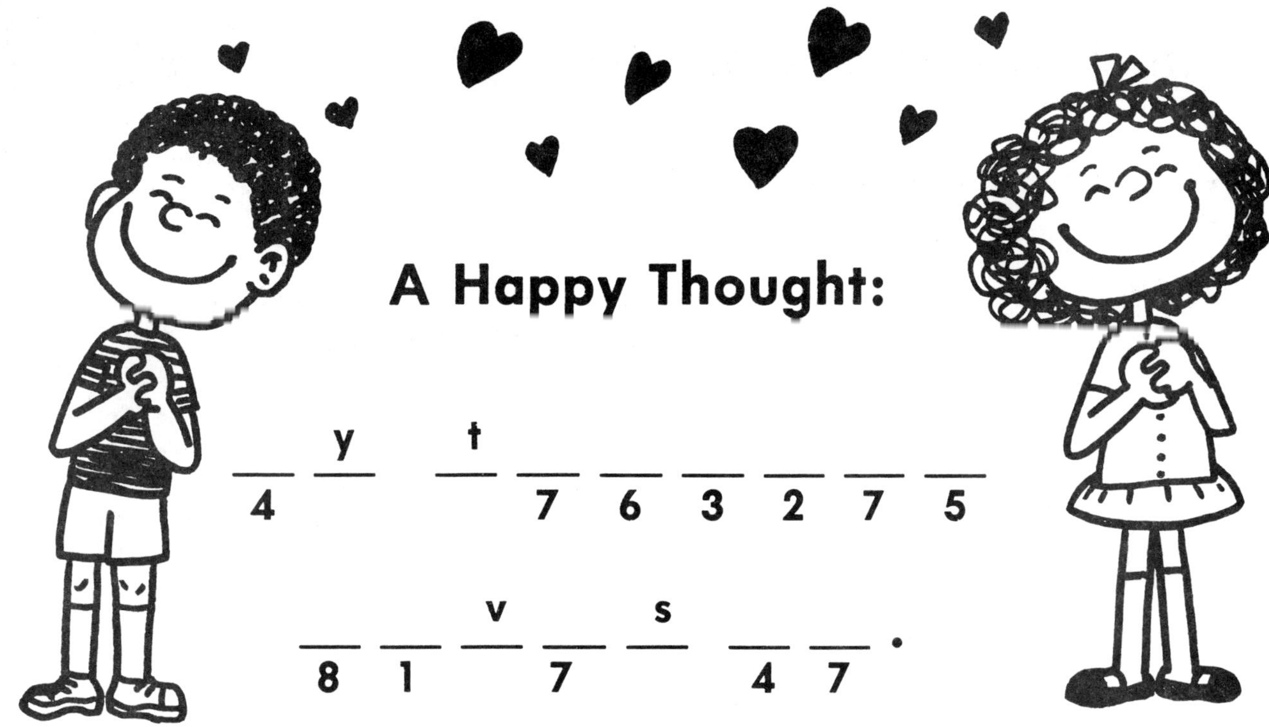

A Happy Thought:

__ y t __ __ __ __ __ __
4 7 6 3 2 7 5

__ __ v __ s __ __.
8 1 7   4 7

1.  m _ p	2.  _ at	3.  _ up	4.  _ en
5.  _ at	6.  b _ t	7.  p _ n	8.  _ og

Name ______________________________

A Riddle:

What animal keeps time best?

I'm never late.

___   ___ ___ ___ ___ ___ ___ ___ ___
1   7 1 6 4 2 5 3 8

1. 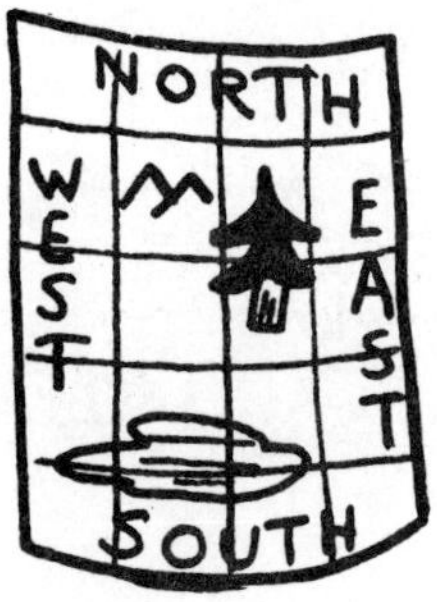
NORTH
WEST
EAST
SOUTH
m __ p

2. 
__ at

3. 
d __ g

4. 
__ up

5. 
be __

6. 
ne__

7. 
__ eb

8. 
ru __

Name________________________________

Nothing!

A Riddle:

What is better than a horse that can count?

__	__	__	__	__	__	__	__	g	__	__	__
5	1	2	6	4	4	3	8		7	6	6

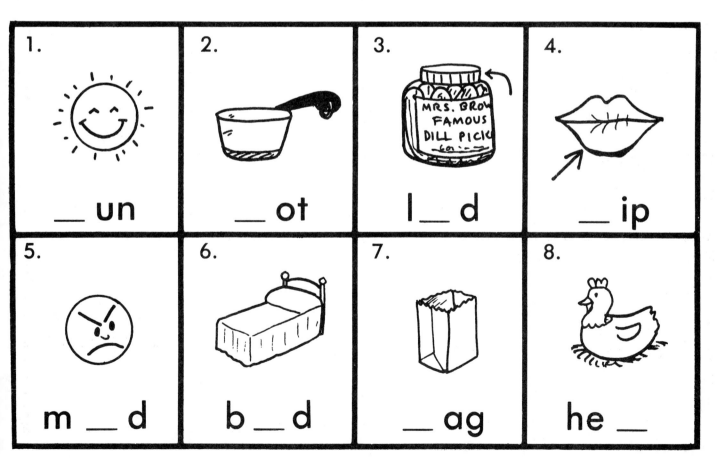

1.	2.	3.	4.
__ un	__ ot	l __ d	__ ip
5.	**6.**	**7.**	**8.**
m __ d	b __ d	__ ag	he __

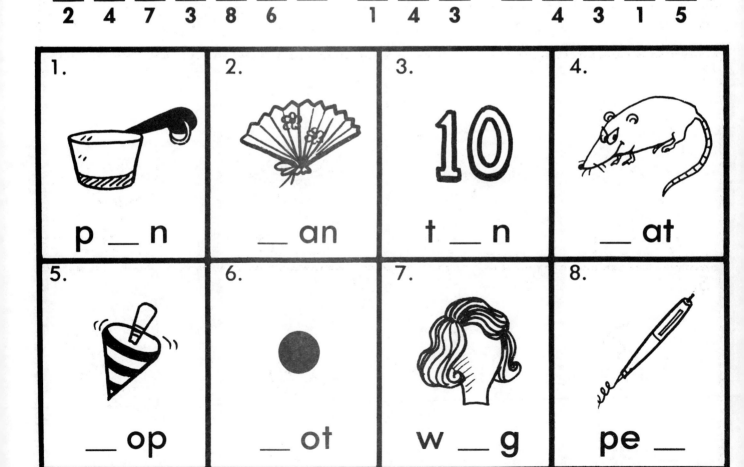

Name ______________________________

Hi ho!
Hi ho!
A Happy Thought:

___ ___ ___ ___ ___ ___ s   ___ ___ ___   g ___ ___ ___ ___ .

2 4 7 3 8 6   1 4 3   4 3 1 5

1.  p __ n	2.  __ an	3.  t __ n	4.  __ at
5.  __ op	6.  __ ot	7.  w __ g	8.  pe __

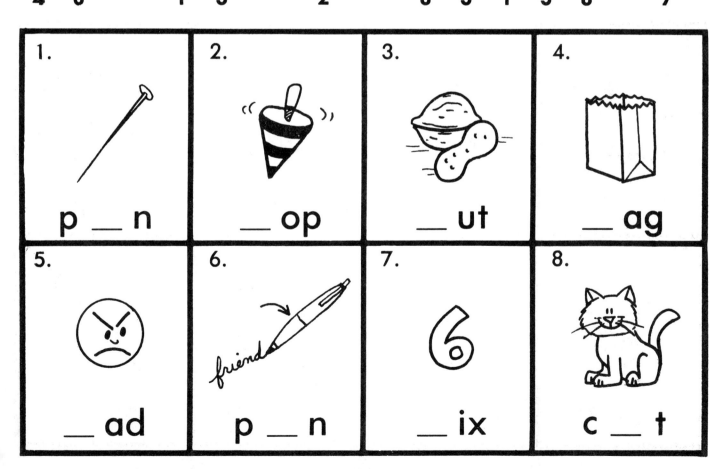

Name ______________________________

...And don't forget!
A Happy Thought:

__	__	k	__	__	d	__	o	__	__	__	__	__	l	__ .
4	6		1	3		2		8	3	1	5	8		7

1. 
p __ n

2. 
__ op

3. 
__ ut

4. 
__ ag

5. 
__ ad

6. 
friend
p __ n

7. 
__ ix

8. 
c __ t

Name ____

scratch
scratch
itch
itch

A Riddle:

What did the dog say to the flea?

___ ___ ___ 't ___ ___ ___ ___ ___ !
8 3 1   5 2 7   6 4

1.  TOMATO ca ___	2.  dr ___ m	3.  fr ___ g	4.  dr ___ ss
5.  ___ ug	6.  ___ op	7.  pi ___	8.  da ___

Name ____

A Riddle:

Why does a chicken lay an egg?

__	f		s	h	__		__	__	__	__	__	__	__		__	t,
4					7		6	1	2	8	8	7	6		4	

__	t		w	__	__	l	__		b	__	__	__	k	.
4				2	3		6			1	7	5		

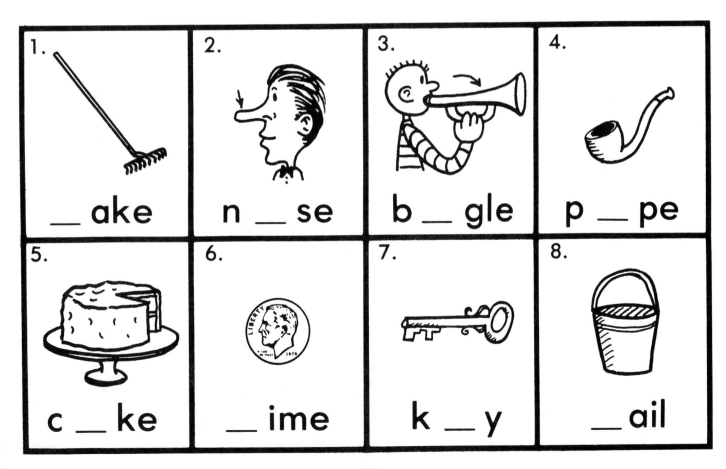

1.  __ ake	2.  n __ se	3.  b __ gle	4.  p __ pe
5.  c __ ke	6.  __ ime	7.  k __ y	8.  __ ail

Name________________________________

Call the custodian!

A Tongue Twister:

T	h	_		_	_	g		_	_	_		_	_	_	_	_	_
		4		8	2			8	4	4		8	3	5	5	4	7

_	y		t	h	_		_	l	_	c	k	_	_	_	r	_	.
8					4		8		6			8	1	6		7	

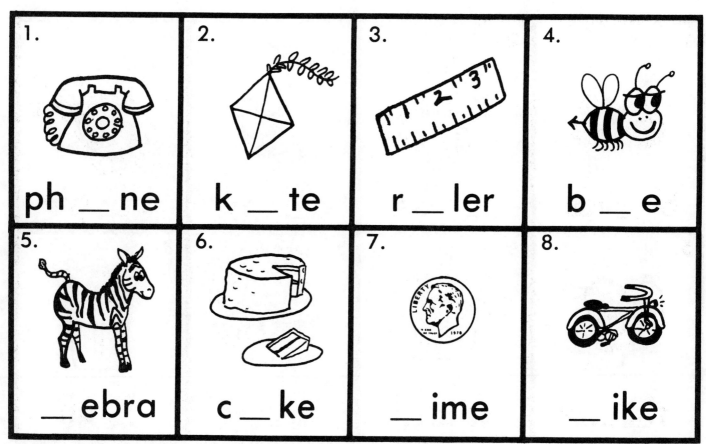

1.	2.	3.	4.
ph __ ne	k __ te	r __ ler	b __ e
5.	**6.**	**7.**	**8.**
__ ebra	c __ ke	__ ime	__ ike

Name ____________________

A Riddle:

Why does a dog wag his tail?

swish

b __ c __ __ s __   __ __   __ __ __
(blanks numbered: 5, 6, 4, 5   8, 3   3, 8, 5)

__ __ s __   __ __ __ __   __ __ g   __ t
(blanks numbered: 5, 2, 5   7, 1, 2, 2   7, 6   1)

f __ r   h __ m
(blanks numbered: 3   1)

1.  b __ ke	2.  __ eash	3.  c __ ne	4.  b __ gle
5.  3 thr __ e	6.  sn __ il	7.  __ ave	8.  __ ail

Name ______________________________

A Riddle: What did the leopard say when it started to rain ?

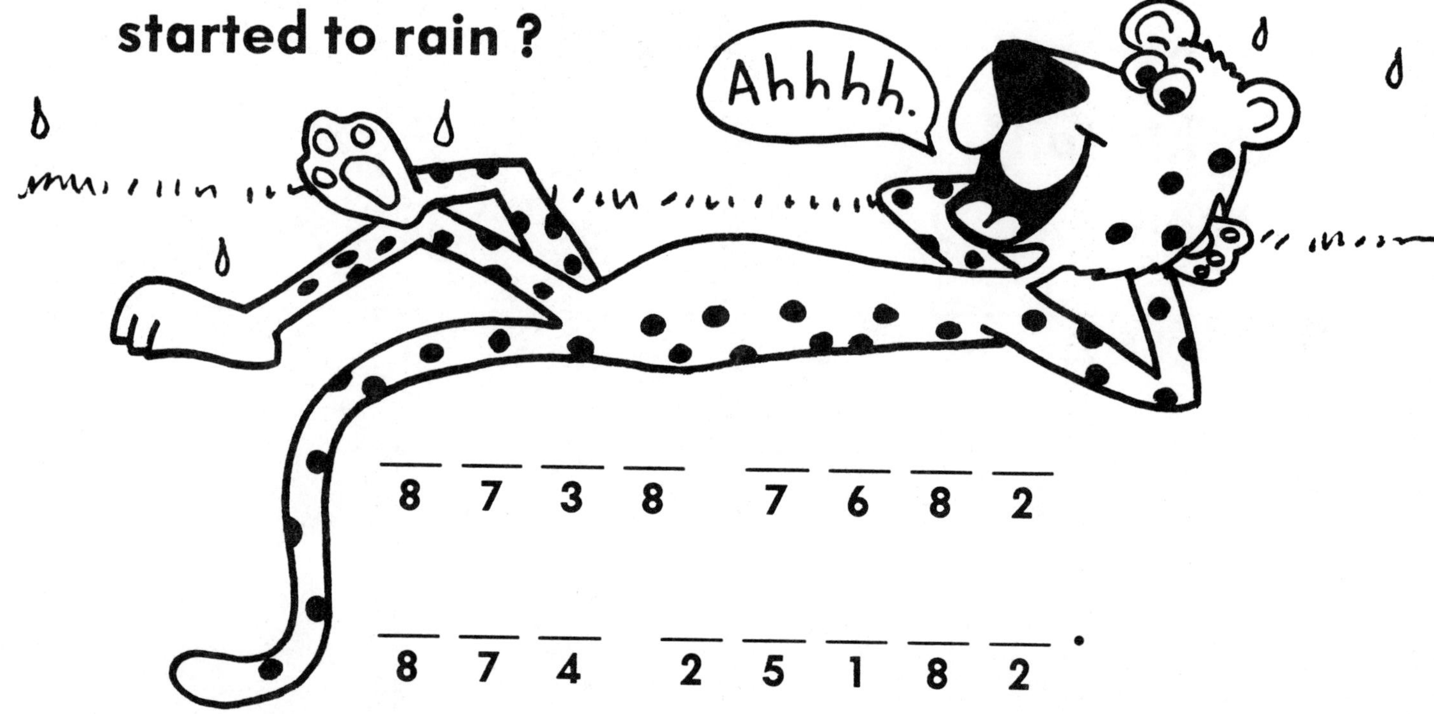
Ahhhh.

_ _ _ _   _ _ _ _
8 7 3 8   7 6 8 2

_ _ _   _ _ _ _ _ .
8 7 4   2 5 1 8 2

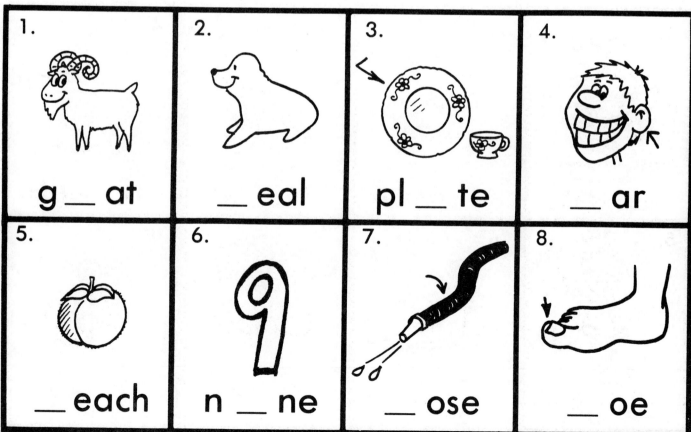

1. g __ at	2. __ eal	3. pl __ te	4. __ ar
5. __ each	6. n __ ne	7. __ ose	8. __ oe

Name ______________________________

... Can't catch me!

A Riddle:

What insect goes skin diving?

___ ___ ___   ___ ___ ___ q ___ ___ ___ ___

5 4 8   1 3 6   7 2 5 3

1.  __ ice	2.  f __ ve	3. 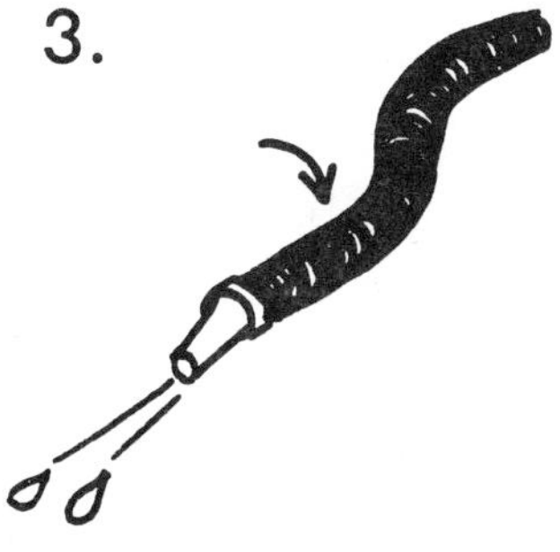 h __ se	4.  __ eel
5.  __ iger	6.  __ eal	7.  fr __ it	8.  b __ e

Name____

A Happy Thought:

__	h	__		__	__	__		__	__	__	l	__		g	__	__	__.
7		2		5	3	8		4	2	2		5			6	6	1

1.	2.	3.	4.
 GO	 z z z z		
__ ice	sl __ ep	b __ gle	lea __
5.	**6.**	**7.**	**8.**

__nail	gh __ st	ki __ e	co __ e

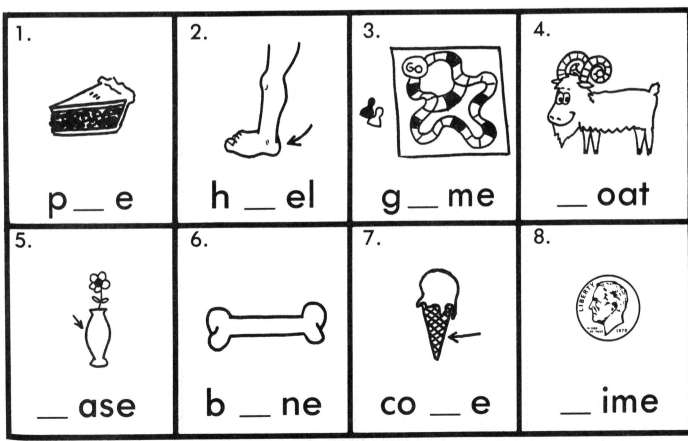

Name ______________________________

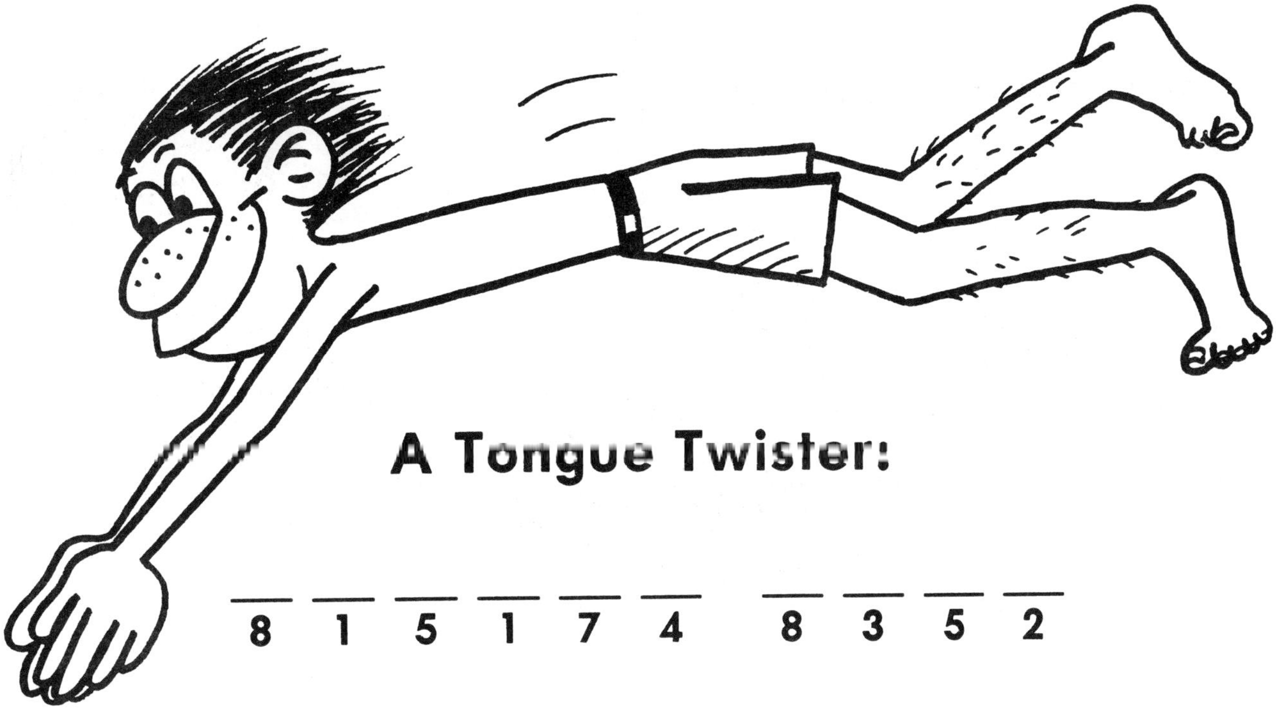

A Tongue Twister:

___ ___ ___ ___ ___ ___   ___ ___ ___ ___
8 1 5 1 7 4   8 3 5 2

___ ___ ___ ___   ___ ___ _w_ ___   ___ ___ ___ _p_ .
8 6 5 2   8 6 7   8 2 2

1.  p __ e	2.  h __ el	3.  g __ me	4.  __ oat
5.  __ ase	6.  b __ ne	7. 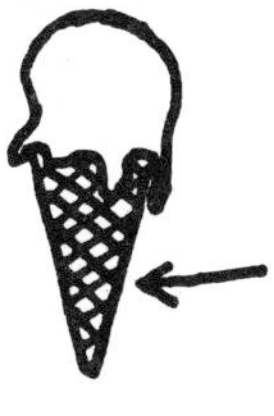 co __ e	8.  __ ime

Name____

A Riddle:

What is the best way to talk to a monster?

..Now don't be afraid.

__	__	__	g		__	__	s	t	__	__	__	__
4	1	6			8	2			3	6	5	7

1.	2.	3.	4.
g __ at	b __ ke	b __ by	__ eaf
5.	**6.**	**7.**	**8.**
__ one	__ ail	b __ e	__ ime

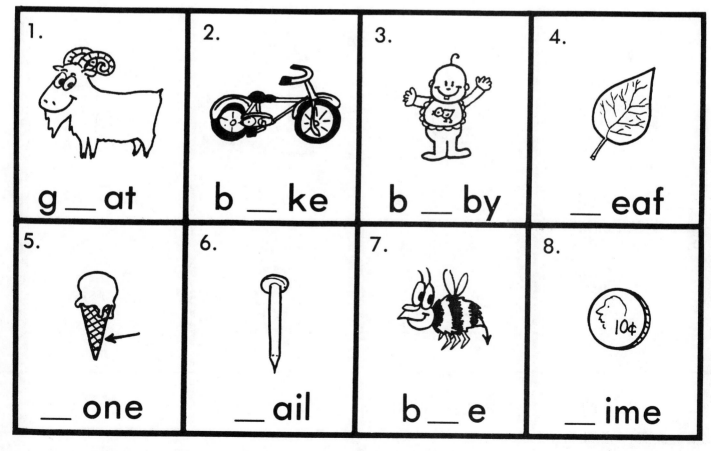

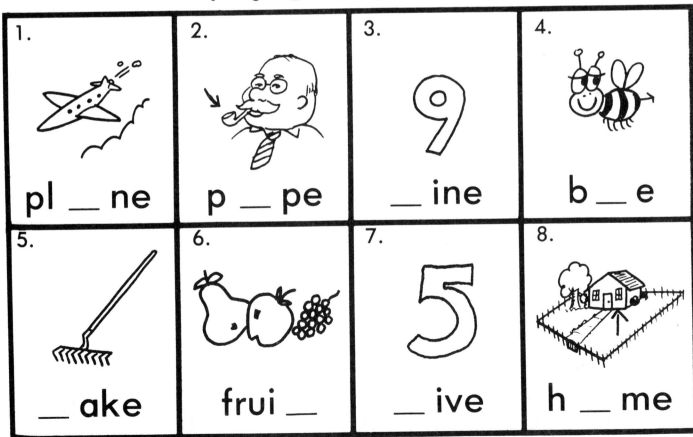

Name ______________________________

A Happy Thought:

___ ___ ___'s ___ ___ c ___ ___ ___ h ___ v ___
(2) (6) ( ) (3) (2) ( ) (4) (6) (8) ( ) (1) ( ) (4)

___ ___ ___ ___ ___ d s .
(7) (5) (2) (4) (3)

1.  pl __ ne	2.  p __ pe	3.  __ ine	4.  b __ e
5.  __ ake	6.  frui __	7.  __ ive	8.  h __ me

Name ____________________

Eeeeeek!

A Riddle:

What do you call a scared fish?

__	__	__	__	k	__	__		__	__		t	__	__		s	__	__
7	8	2	7		1	5		3	4			8	1			1	6

1.  __ ar	2.  t __ e	3.  b __ ne	4. 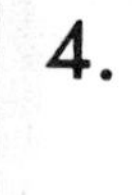 __ ive
5.  __ ail	6. snail picture sn __ il	7.  __ ake	8.  __ ome

Name ____

Daffynition:

Kitchen

sprinkle
sprinkle
S

__   __ __ __ __ __   __ __ __
8   1 2 8 5 7   8 4 3

b __ __ __   __ l __ c __
  8 5 7   6   8   7

1.  __ nail	2.  __ ome	3.  __ ime	4.   pla __ e
5.  __ ite	6.  __ ie	7.  t __ eth	8.  t __ pe

Name ____________________

A Happy Thought:

Help keep the world beautiful! Do your part. Hurray!

D __ n' __ __ __ __
  7   3   6 2 5

__ __ __ __ __ r __ __ g .
1 4 3 3 2   6 8

1.	2.	3.	4.
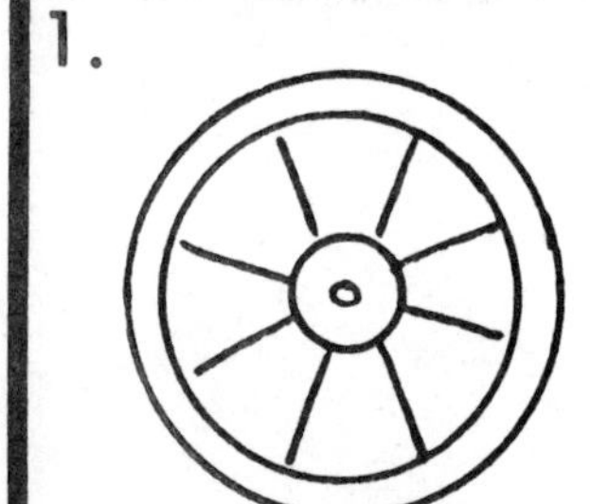			
whee__	sh __ ep	__ree	sm __ le
5.	6.	7.	8.
		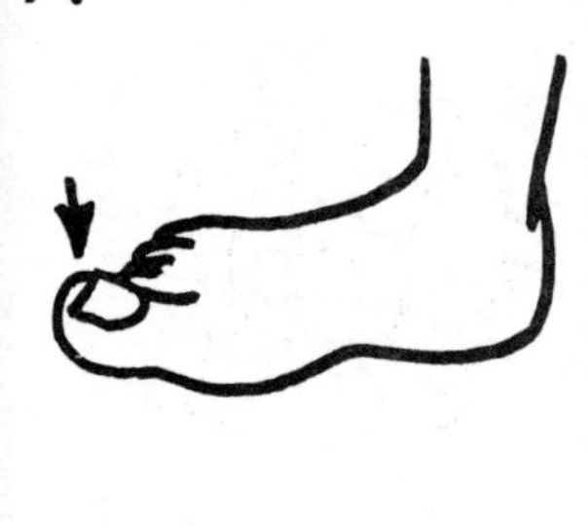	
tr __ in	__ low	t __ e	b __ gle

Name ______________________________

I guess you start with sugar...

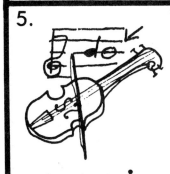

A Riddle:

How do you make a lemon drop?

J ___ ___ ___   ___ ___ ___   ___ ___   ___ ___ ___ ___ .

    5 6 7   4 3 7   1 7   8 2 4 4

1.  m __ ce	2.  ch __ in	3.  k __ y	4.  __ eaf
5.  m __ sic	6.  __ nail	7.  __ ire	8.  __ ruit

Name ______________________________

I'll get it!

A Riddle:

What is black and white and lives in San Diego?

___		___	___	___	t		___	___	___	g	u	___	___
3		1	2	8			6	7	4			5	4

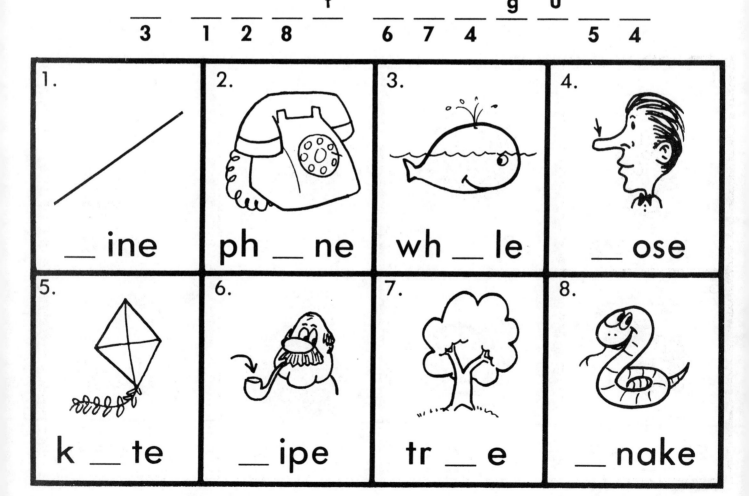

1. ___ ine	2. ph ___ ne	3. wh ___ le	4. ___ ose
5. k ___ te	6. ___ ipe	7. tr ___ e	8. ___ nake

Name ______________________________

A Happy Thought:

___   ___ m ___ l ___   ___ ___   ___   g ___ ___ ___ ___

1   8   2   3   2 8   1   4 3 1 7

w ___ ___   ___ ___   ___ ___ ___ ___ ___

1 6   7 5   8 7 1 4 7

___ h ___   d ___ ___ .

7   3   1 6

1.  v __ se	2.  t __ re	3.  b __ e	4.  __ ake
5.  st __ ve	6.  __ o-yo	7.  __ iger	8.  __ nake

Name ______________________________

WHAMO

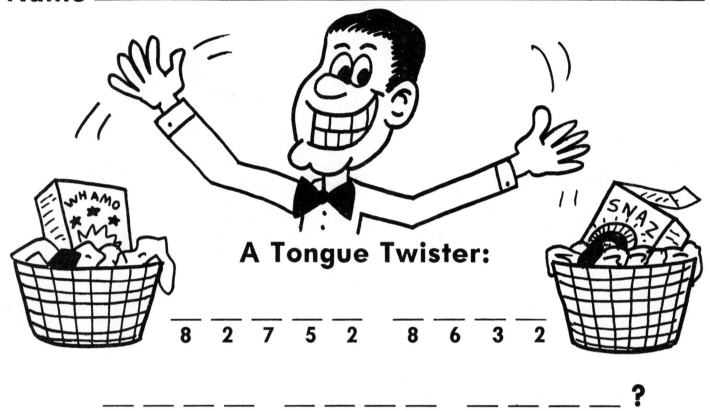

A Tongue Twister:

__ __ __ __ __ __ __ __ __
8 2 7 5 2 8 6 3 2

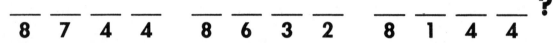

__ __ __ __ __ __ __ __ __ __ __ __ ?
8 7 4 4 8 6 3 2 8 1 4 4

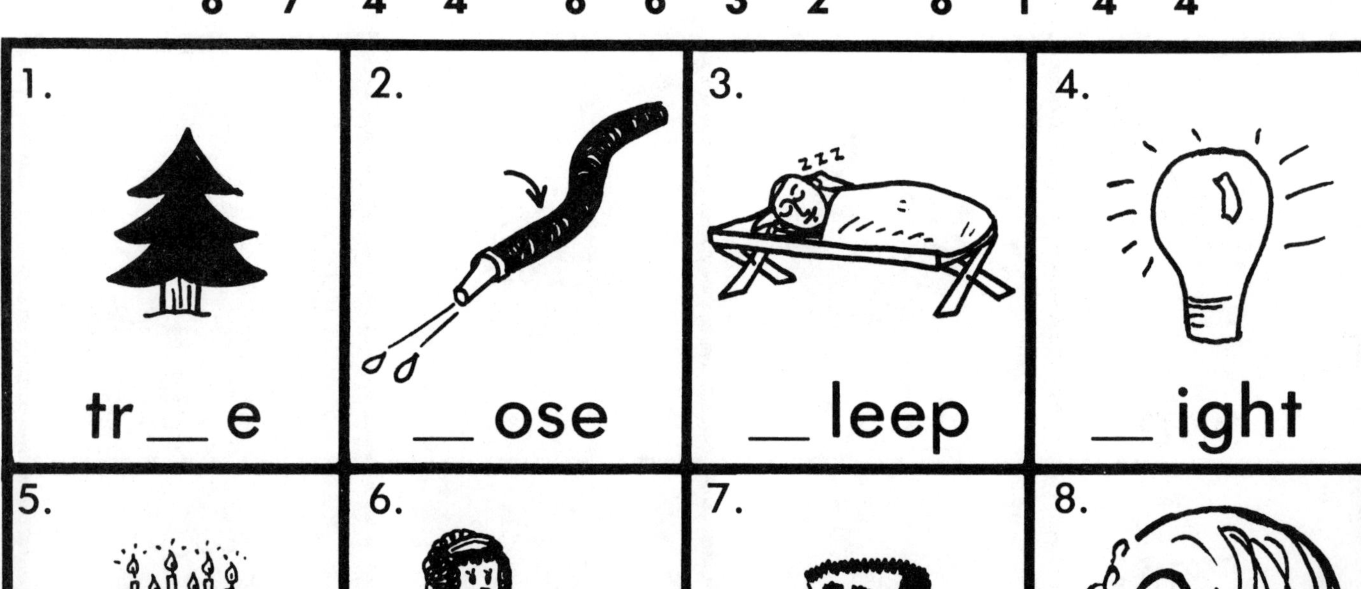

1.  tr __ e	2. 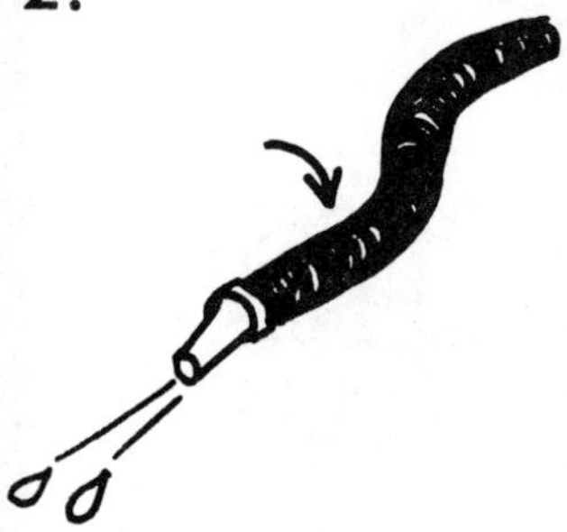 __ ose	3.  __ leep	4.  __ ight
5.  __ ake	6.  tr __ y	7.  sm __ le	8.  __ ave

Name ________________________________

A Riddle:

What is worse than finding a worm in an apple?

__ __ __ __   __   __ __ __ __

1 4 5 8   4   7 3 6 2

1.  __ ose	2.  __ ail	3.  FRAGILE h __ me	4.  t __ ble
5.  __ eaf	6.  __ uler	7.  __ eep	8.  __ ive

Name ______________________________

I don't
know.

A Riddle:

What is the biggest diamond in the world?

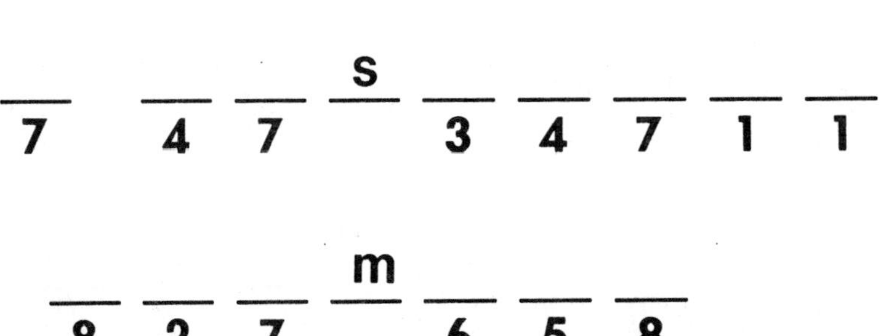

___   ___ ___ s ___ ___ ___ ___ ___

7   4 7   3 4 7 1 1

___ ___ ___ m ___ ___ ___

8 2 7   6 5 8

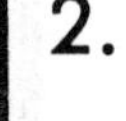

1.	2.	3.	4.

__ ight	p __ pe	__ ar	__ one
5.	**6.**	**7.**	**8.**

__ ose	c __ ne	r __ ke	__ ime

10¢

Name ______________________________

A Happy Thought:

H __ __ __ __ __ s __
(2 8 8 1 3 6)

k __ __ __ w __ __ __ .
(3 7 4 1 5 4)

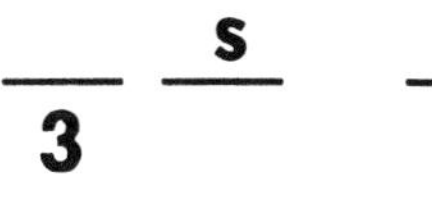

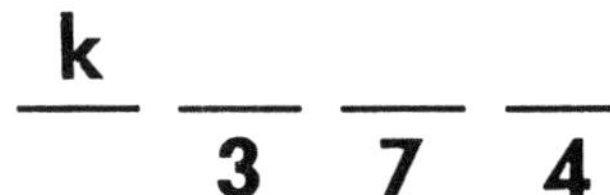

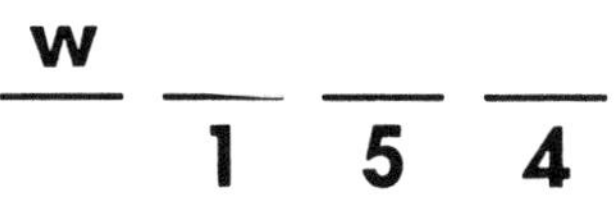

1. n __ te	2. thr __ e	3. t __ e	4. __ ime
5. __ ake	6. c __ ge	7. li __ e	8. __ eaf

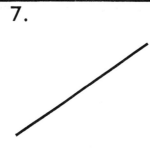

Name ______________________________

She sounds cute.

A Riddle:

What is brown and blue

and has green teeth

and a red nose.

	h						s							
8		2	5	2		6			7	3	2		7	3

y							m	.
	7	1	5		4	5		

1.	2.	3.	4.
b __ gle	j __ ep	__ ail	pl __ ne

5.	6.	7.	8.
__ ake	b __ ke	b __ at	__ ree

Name ______________________________ Skill: Phonics, Visual discrimination

Read the words in the Word Box.
Write the word that completes each sentence.
Circle the words in the puzzle.

1. I ______________ to play ball soon.
2. ______________ are they coming?
3. ______________ is that man over there?
4. He ______________ home.
5. ______________ is his name?
6. ______________ did he go after school?
7. I wonder ______________ I'm hungry?
8. ______________ dog is yours?

Word Box

went
want
where
when
what
who
why
which

l	w	h	e	r	e	w
w	a	s	w	h	o	h
h	n	w	e	n	t	i
a	t	h	w	h	y	c
t	t	w	h	e	n	h

Name ______________________________ Skill: Phonics, Reading comprehension

Read the words in the Word Box.
Write the word that completes each sentence.
Circle the words in the puzzle.

1. I want ____________ to go.
2. Where did ____________ go?
3. Two is more ____________ one.
4. ____________ is the one I want.
5. I live ____________.
6. Get your book, ____________ we will read.
7. This is ____________ new car.
8. Do you ____________ you can go?

Word Box
this
they
than
then
them
there
their
think

l	s	t	h	e	r	e
t	t	h	i	s	t	t
t	h	e	m	m	h	h
q	h	y	p	d	e	i
n	a	t	h	a	n	n
t	h	e	i	r	l	k

Name ____________________ Skill: **ch**, **sh**

The New House

Word Box
- orchard
- fishing
- beach
- share
- shop
- shady
- bench
- patch
- charge
- cherry

s	c	p	l	o	c	a	l	n	k
h	h	t	s	r	b	e	n	c	h
o	a	a	d	c	r	t	z	a	m
p	r	r	r	h	a	p	n	a	g
m	g	p	l	a	q	l	s	i	m
t	e	a	g	r	h	l	h	x	b
s	e	t	n	d	s	h	a	r	e
p	l	c	a	e	h	s	d	m	a
l	c	h	e	r	r	y	y	i	c
f	i	s	h	i	n	g	n	l	h

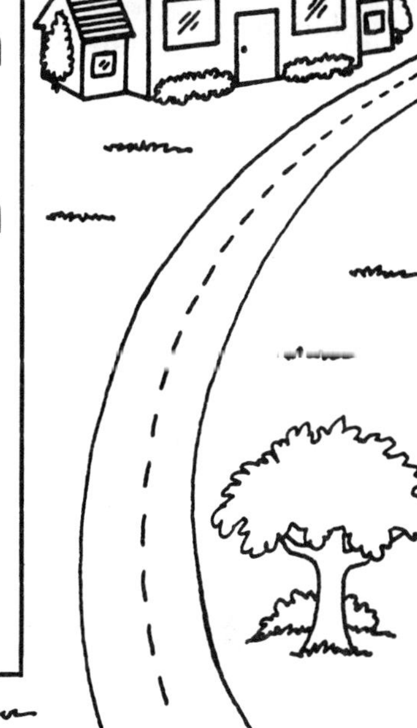

1. The new house I just moved into has a large back yard filled with ____________ trees.
2. I enjoy sitting on a ____________ under a tree and reading a book.
3. The trees keep the sun out and make our yard very ____________.
4. I also like the strawberry ____________ next to the garden.
5. I am in ____________ of picking the berries.
6. After I pick them, I like to ____________ some of them with my new friends.
7. There is a beautiful sandy ____________ close to my new house.
8. When I go there, I can either swim or go ____________ off the pier.
9. A few blocks from my house is a ____________ that carries interesting games and puzzles.
10. I like my new house and everything around it, but I think I like my cherry tree ____________ best.

Name ____________________ Skill: **gh, ph**

Under the Weather

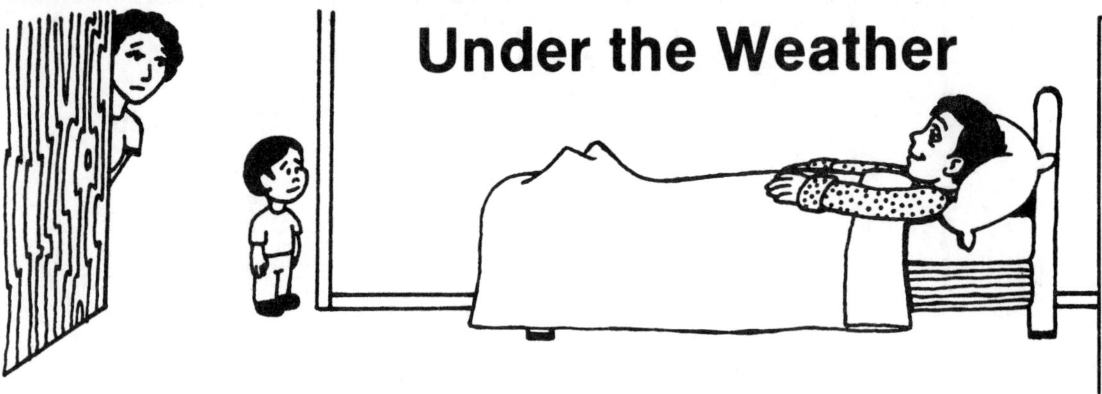

Word Box
caught
cough
flight
tough
laugh
telephone
alphabet
neighbor
elephant
freight

1. Matt had a very bad ____________.
2. He had ____________ a cold and cough from his best friend Jon.
3. The day he got it, he and Jon had been racing to see who could write all the letters of the ____________ faster.
4. Even though Jon was his next-door ____________, Matt couldn't see Jon again until they were both well.
5. Matt did call Jon and talk to him on the ____________.
6. It was ____________ not being able to see his best friend.
7. Matt was bored, so he let his imagination take ____________.
8. He pretended he was traveling in a ____________ train in a far-away country.
9. He passed a huge, grey ____________ lumbering along.
10. It made him ____________ when he found out that Jon had been using his imagination to make up adventures, too.

p	e	f	c	a	u	g	h	t	y
r	l	q	m	l	b	r	l	c	n
t	e	l	e	p	h	o	n	e	e
f	p	a	s	h	v	d	t	c	i
l	h	u	m	a	h	p	o	o	g
i	a	g	d	b	g	q	u	u	h
g	n	h	d	e	u	v	g	g	b
h	t	q	i	t	o	y	h	h	o
t	e	v	r	z	r	k	p	q	r
g	f	r	e	i	g	h	t	r	h

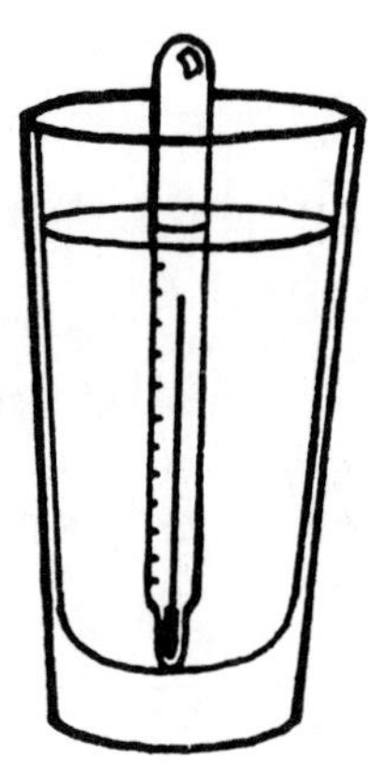

Name ________________________________

AR park **OR** horn

Write the name of the picture on the line.

______

______

______

______

RUFF!
______

RRRIPP!
______

HONK!
______

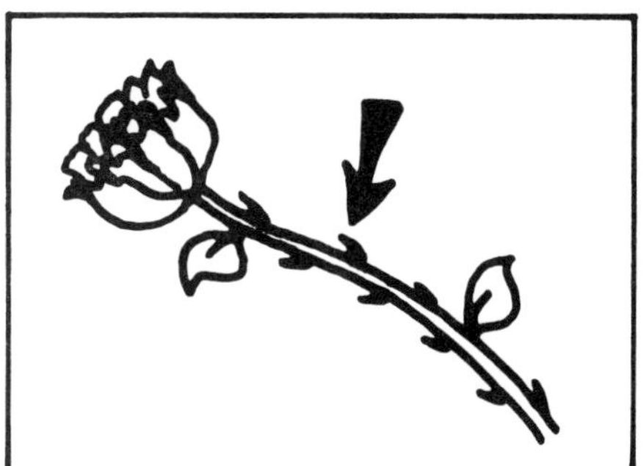
______

______

______

______

______

Name ______________________________

OR	UR	AR
horn	turn	park

Circle the word that has the same R-sound as the picture. The first one is done for you.

1. Cows sleep in a .	her	 hard	stir
2. Go to the GENERAL.	mark	first	horse
3. Use my .	smart	port	hurry
4. I love .	for	start	dirt
5. Jam comes in a 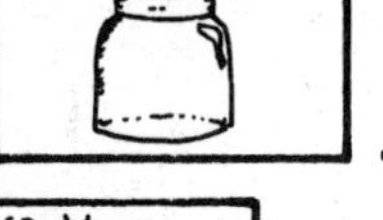.	pork	art	her
6. Your dress is .	turn	park	pork
7. My sister is a 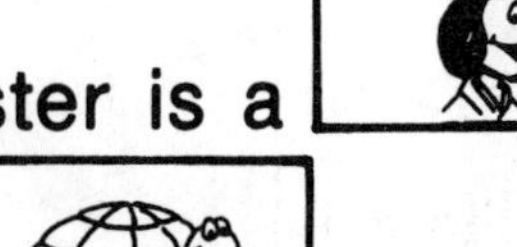.	purple	dark	fork
8. Our  can swim.	barn	port	hurt
9. Father is cooking a 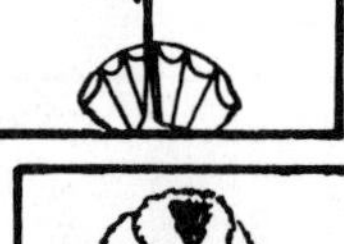.	fur	horse	party
10. Mother is wearing a  coat.	farm	torn	hurry
11. Did you cut your ?	turn	park	pork
12. Sue sent me a birthday HAPPY BIRTHDAY.	dark	curl	stir

Name ____________________

ER	UR	IR
silver	turtle	girl

Circle the words that have the same R-sound as the picture.

corn
burn
dinner
car
teacher
hurry
third

surprise
skirt
start
horse
jar
rubber
barn

RN
RN

her
pork
turn
park
bird
girl
morning

Write the name of the picture. Use the words in the boxes above for clues.

1.
8+9 =17
2.
3.
4.
5.
6.

1. ____________
2. ____________
3. ____________
4. ____________
5. ____________
6. ____________

Read the clues. Choose the word from the list that best fits each clue.

1. swings, grass ____________
2. season, cold ____________
3. clowns, tent ____________
4. coin, shiny ____________
5. nest, wings ____________
6. cows, hay ____________

bird	silver
circus	bride
barn	sir
park	burn
winter	water
wonder	

Name ______________________________

UR	IR	ER
turn	first	dinner

Complete each sentence with the correctly spelled word.
The picture above will give you some clues.

1. The ball is made of ______________ .
   rubbar rubber rubbor

2. Becky is wearing a long ______________ .
   skirt skort skart

3. A big ______________ is sitting near the pond.
   tortle turtle tartle

4. What kind of ______________ is that?
   bord bard bird

5. The ______________ is a very tall man.
   farmer former firmer

6. Becky is feeding a ______________ .
   tarkey turkey torkey

7. A small butterfly is on Mr. Mann's ______________ .
   short shart shirt

8. Mr. Mann is carrying a ______________ and some wood.
   hammer hammor hammar

9. Becky is a little __________ . Her hair has no __________ .
   garl gorl girl **curl carl corl**

Name ______________________________________

AR	ER	IR	UR	OR
park	dinner	first	turn	horn

Read each clue. Find the answer in the list below. Write your answer on the line.

1. a food that is yellow ____________
2. something you eat on Thanksgiving ____________
3. a warm season ____________
4. a place to keep jam ____________
5. something to wear ____________
6. the opposite of south ____________
7. a sound made by a dog ____________
8. where to see a clown ____________
9. someone who plows ____________
10. a dark color ____________
11. a round shape ____________
12. a time of day ____________

farmer	bark	turkey	purple
morning	corn	circle	circus
jar	north	shirt	summer

Name ______________________________

AR	IR	ER	UR	OR
park	first	dinner	turn	horn

Read each sentence. Choose the word that best completes the sentence and write it on the line.

1. Some cows live in a __________
   barn born burn
2. I'm going to be in the __________ grade.
   thorn turn third
3. If you don't __________, we'll be late.
   hurry harry hurt
4. __________ is my favorite vegetable.
   core card corn
5. Did the house __________ down?
   born bore burn
6. At night, it is very __________ .
   dart dark dirt
7. Tim fell and __________ his knee.
   hard herb hurt
8. Take this pen and give it to __________ .
   her hare hire
9. A __________ crawls very slowly.
   turkey teacher turtle
10. Meat from pigs is called __________ .
    port park pork
11. Let's have a __________ party for Anne.
    silver smart surprise
12. Don't swim out too __________ !
    fur first far

Name ________________________________

Write the name of the picture on the line.

1.
2.
HONK!
3.
4.
5.
6.

1. ____________
2. ____________
3. ____________
4. ____________
5. ____________
6. ____________

Circle the words that have the same R-sound as the picture.

her
barn
hurt
corn
far
first

HONK!

hammer
start
pork
thorn
turn
horse

dark
burn
party
north
shirt
card

Write the word that best completes the sentence.

4. Would you like ____________ for dinner?
   torkey tarkey turkey

5. Let's go to the ____________ and play.
   pork park perk

6. My little ____________ is three years old.
   sistor sistar sister

7. Lynn won ____________ prize!
   third thord thard

8. The school ____________ will take care of me.
   norse nurse narse

Name ______________________________ Skill: **ar**

Our School Carnival

Central School
Carnival
March 8, 1994 3-9:00 P.M.
326 $5.00

326

1. Each ____________ we have a school carnival at Central School.
2. Everyone joins in on the fun of ____________ for this special night.
3. ____________ make baked goods for us to sell.
4. We ____________ money for the tickets to this fund-raising event.
5. A ____________ number of people always turn out for this fun evening.
6. The fifth graders run the ____________ throw.
7. There is an ____________ who does face painting.
8. The ____________ haunted house is a favorite activity for everyone.
9. We plan to use a large ____________ of the money we make to buy more playground equipment.
10. Wouldn't you like to come to the Central School ____________?

w	a	p	x	M	l	c	p	y	c
v	r	r	y	a	a	h	r	m	a
u	t	e	a	r	t	a	s	b	r
p	i	p	r	c	g	r	t	u	n
a	s	a	o	h	x	g	l	e	i
r	t	r	r	w	i	e	a	h	v
e	d	i	a	s	h	a	r	e	a
n	a	n	h	z	e	r	g	u	l
t	r	g	s	q	a	r	e	i	t
s	t	d	a	r	k	e	n	e	d

Word Box

darkened
large
parents
preparing
March
carnival
share
artist
charge
dart

Name ______________________________ Skill: **er**, **ir**, **ur**

School Lunches

1. Every day different food is ____________________ in the lunch room.
2. Monday is ____________________ -on-a-bun day and my favorite day.
3. The best thing about lunch on Tuesday is that our room goes through the lunch line ____________________.
4. The spaghetti on Wednesday is not my favorite because I like my mom's spaghetti ____________________.
5. On ____________________, lunch at school is best.
6. It's difficult for me to wait my ____________________ in line then.
7. Thursday we always have ____________________ with mashed potatoes and gravy.
8. On Friday, we have ____________________ cooked in lemon butter.
9. To end our lunch each day, we have ____________________.
10. My favorite dessert is apple ____________________.

Word Box

perch
first
served
better
dessert
turn
hamburger
cobbler
turkey
Thursday

T	c	o	b	b	l	e	r	n	f
p	h	w	t	h	e	e	t	i	i
e	t	u	r	n	b	r	t	f	r
r	e	y	r	b	e	m	u	i	s
c	n	o	p	s	i	e	r	b	t
h	e	r	s	r	d	v	k	e	i
i	v	e	n	i	g	a	e	t	e
l	d	k	i	n	t	e	y	t	c
o	h	a	m	b	u	r	g	e	r
s	e	r	v	e	d	l	o	r	d

Name ________________________ Skill: Phonics, —oo vowel diagraph

Read the words in the Word Box.
Write the word that completes each sentence.
Circle the words in the puzzle.

1. I like to dive into the swimming ________________.
2. My favorite ________________ is pizza.
3. Do you like to look at the ________________ at night?
4. I bought a red ________________ at the circus.
5. The funniest animals in the ________________ are the monkeys.
6. Very ________________ it will be summer vacation.
7. What do you like best in ________________?
8. Mother said I could go, ________________.

Word Box			
food	balloon	too	soon
zoo	pool	moon	school

b	a	l	l	o	o	n	s
s	p	o	o	l	o	m	o
c	l	n	l	s	t	u	o
h	z	o	o	m	o	a	n
o	o	f	o	o	d	c	y
o	o	y	h	o	o	z	g
l	p	e	c	n	c	h	o
l	o	v	s	h	t	o	o

Name ________________________________

oo moon | oo look

Read the sentences. Write the last words in the correct order.

1. Phil went to ____________________ . at noon school
2. Sit down and ____________________ . book at look the
3. Sara has ____________________ . tooth a loose
4. Do you think the ____________________ ? cookies good are
5. Look! There's a ____________________ ! pool goose in the

Write the word from the list that best completes each sentence.

1. Come over and swim in our __________ .
2. Jan is wearing a warm __________ coat.
3. You'll need a __________ for your soup.
4. These chairs are made of __________ .
5. If it rains, put on your __________ .
6. Wait for your __________ to __________ before you eat it.

spoon
wood
pool
boots
cool
wool
food

Name ______________________________ Skill: **oo**

A Walk in the Woods

1. Sarah and Kristin enjoy following the ______________ path through the woods on their way to school.
2. On the way home they often stop and sit by the ______________ to talk.
3. The water looks so ______________ as it ripples over the rocks.
4. Some days they even pack extra ______________ so they can eat a snack on their way home.
5. While they are sitting eating, they often see a furry ______________ run across a log near them.
6. The girls love the ______________ because it is peaceful there.
7. In the morning, they make sure they don't spend ______________ much time there because they don't want to be late for school.
8. ______________ it will be summer and the girls can spend as much time in the woods as they want to.
9. They will pack their lunches, take along a good ______________ or two to read, and spend the whole day by the brook.
10. But today is a ______________ day, so they have to be on their way.

w	b	s	o	o	n	f	s	t	c
s	o	p	x	z	f	g	b	b	r
f	g	o	x	u	e	c	r	o	o
o	h	f	d	b	b	o	o	k	o
o	i	x	w	s	a	o	o	o	k
d	s	c	h	o	o	l	k	o	e
t	w	s	r	x	r	h	m	p	d
o	n	r	a	c	c	o	o	n	t
o	l	q	v	a	b	j	k	m	v

Word Box

school
brook
food
woods
soon
too
book
crooked
cool
raccoon

Name ______________________________

The vowels **AU** and **AW** make a single sound. Say these words:

c**au**ght y**aw**n

Read the sentences. Write the last words in the correct order.

1. Dan wakes up at ______________ . yawns and dawn
2. My dog has ______________ . on paws claws his
3. Linda is the name ______________ . my daughter of
4. No one knows how ______________ . caught Paul cold a
5. Can you ______________ ? a hawk draw

My Pa has claws!

Write the word from the list that best completes each sentence.

6. The month after July is __________ .
7. Lynn can't go with us __________ she is sick.
8. On Sunday, Dad mows the __________ .
9. The season of fall is also called __________ .
10. Would you please __________ me a picture?

paw
autumn
draw
August
because
lawn
auto

Name ______________________

AW	AU	OO	OO
yawn	caught	book	moon

Find the word that matches each picture. Circle it.

1. 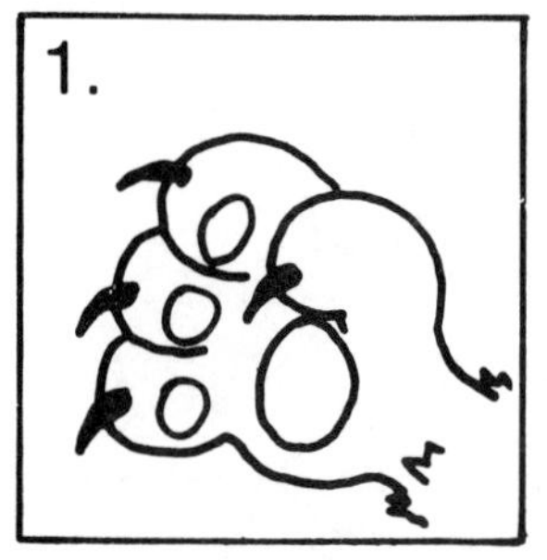
clam
clock
claw
clay

5. 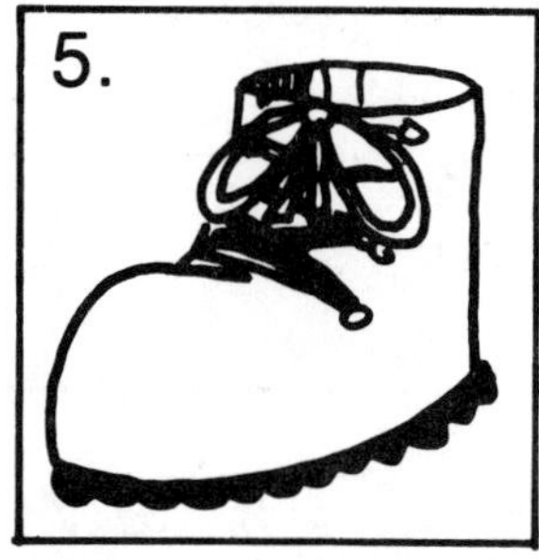
bowl
boom
boat
boot

9. 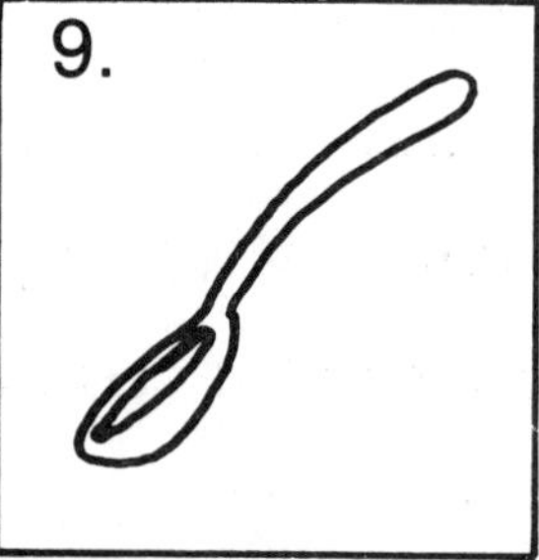
spool
spoon
spend
spine

2. 
OOO12
aunt
auto
apart
ate

6. 
yes
yarn
yawn
yard

10. 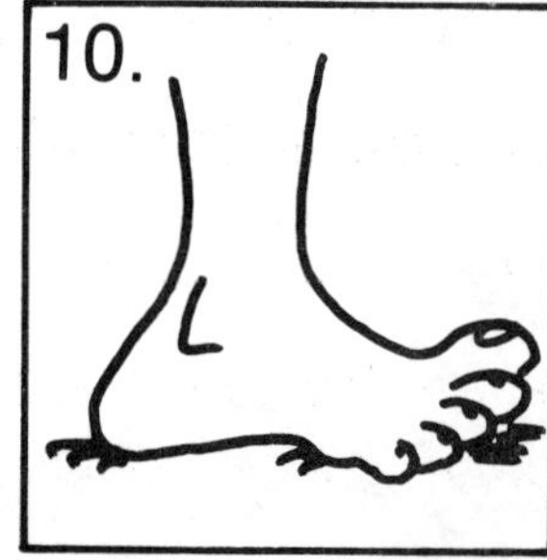
fate
foot
food
fool

3. 
dinner
daughter
dinosaur
driver

7. 
cork
cake
cool
cook

11. 
jaw
jam
jar
jay

4. 
tooth
tote
tool
toast

8. 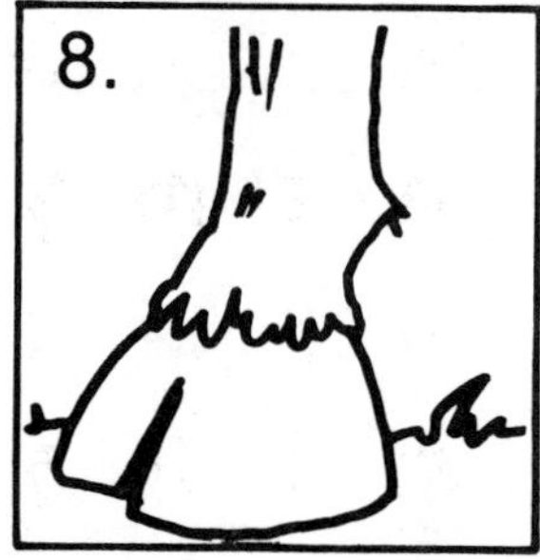
half
hoot
heap
hoof

12. 
dawn
dryer
drain
draw

What comes next? Choose your answers from the words you have circled above.

13. knife, fork, ____________

14. toe, heel, ____________

15. cheek, chin, ____________

16. mother, sister, ____________

Name ____ Skill: **aw**, **al**

Baby-sitting

1. Rob is a very good baby-sitter for ____________________ children.
2. He makes sure the babies have a safe place to ____________________ around.
3. Children who are learning to walk sometimes move in an ____________________ way, so Rob makes sure they don't fall.
4. He likes to listen to young children ____________________.
5. He teaches the children to ____________________ pictures.
6. He gives them ____________________ to use on the chalkboard.
7. He takes them for ____________________.
8. On nice days, they all play out on the green ____________________.
9. Playing ____________________ is a fun outdoor game for everyone.
10. Parents who leave their children with Rob never ____________________ to check on them because Rob is a baby-sitter they can trust.

Word Box

lawn
call
small
draw
chalk
walks
awkward
talk
crawl
ball

d	s	m	a	l	l	b	w	e	c
r	i	a	b	v	e	c	o	j	h
a	o	m	d	a	c	a	q	w	a
w	e	t	o	u	l	l	o	e	l
r	v	c	r	a	w	l	d	s	k
y	e	e	t	m	y	i	h	w	h
l	b	s	a	o	s	y	k	a	n
a	h	m	l	h	s	e	n	l	o
w	a	w	k	w	a	r	d	k	s
n	l	a	r	t	e	s	t	s	f

Name ______________________________

The vowels **EW** and **UE** make the same sound. Say these words:

new blue

Read each sentence. Write the last words in the correct order.

1. I know this story ____________ . not is true
2. Please go get ____________ . more screw one
3. You'll need some paper ____________ . some and glue
4. Did you know that ____________ ? likes blue Sue
5. John got the ball and ____________ . me it threw to

Write the word from the list that best completes each sentence.

6. Little kittens cry and ________ .
7. Bobby's word was a good ________ .
8. Babies can't ________ . They don't have teeth.
9. I only have a ________ cookies.
10. The bird ________ through the ________ sky.

knew
blue
few
flew
mew
true
clue
chew

Name ______________________________ Skill: **oo**, **ew**, **ue**, **ui**

Field Trips

1. My name is ______________________ and I'm in the third grade.
2. During the year, my teacher Miss Park takes us on special trips to ____________________ and exciting places.
3. Last week we went to the city ______________________.
4. My favorite animal there is the ______________________.
5. Afterwards, we went to the park, where we ______________________ kites.
6. The wind ______________________ my kite up in a tree.
7. In the fall, the class went to an orchard and picked ______________________ right off the trees.
8. My favorite trip was to a bakery where we each got a ______________________ muffin free.
9. The owner of the bakery gave each of us a ______________________, too.
10. Our party at the end of the year is going to be the most fun of all because Miss Park told us to bring our bathing ______________________.

b	b	k	a	n	g	a	r	o	o
m	l	s	f	x	t	z	o	o	f
j	g	u	l	s	m	l	y	s	r
b	h	p	e	t	b	s	o	t	u
a	r	o	w	b	l	m	p	u	i
l	p	n	u	e	e	l	q	v	t
l	m	S	c	n	w	r	r	w	x
o	l	u	v	e	a	j	r	z	y
o	x	e	w	w	n	i	h	y	f
n	k	s	u	i	t	s	c	d	e

Word Box
- balloon
- suits
- blew
- flew
- zoo
- new
- Sue
- blueberry
- fruit
- kangaroo

Bakery

Name ______________________________

OU	OW
house	down

Read the sentences. Write the last three words in the correct order.

1. This is a funny story ______________________ .mouse about a
2. A toy store is ______________________ . our near house
3. Have you ever seen ______________________ ? a frown cow
4. Bonnie is wearing a ______________________. gown pretty brown
5. Quiet! Don't make ______________________ . sounds any loud

Write the word from the list that best completes each sentence.

1. Let's go to the circus and see the ____________ .
2. Those dark ____________ mean it is going to rain.
3. Chew with your ____________ shut.
4. Yesterday I lost my pen. Today I ____________ it.
5. I like to take a bath, not a ____________ .
6. The king put on his ____________ and went to ____________ .

mouth
town
brown
crown
clouds
house
found
shower
clowns

Name ______________________________ Skill: **ow, ou**

The Mystery Vacation

SOUTH

Word Box
crowd
mountains
around
how
down
south
outside
clouds
loudly
town

1. All Father would tell Mary and Tom about their vacation was that they were going down ____________.
2. They all went ______________ and piled into the car.
3. As Father drove off, he gave them another clue. "We're going ______________ as well as up," he said.
4. "__________ can we do that?" the children wondered.
5. It was ______________ twelve o'clock when they stopped for lunch.
6. When they got back in the car, Mary and Tom fell asleep. Suddenly, they heard horns honking ______________.
7. There were cars everywhere and a large ______________ of people had gathered along the street.
8. As soon as they saw the elephants, Mary and Tom knew the circus had come to __________.
9. They drove right by and went high up into the rugged ______________.
10. As they climbed into the soft ______________, they were happy they had gone down south and up into the mountains.

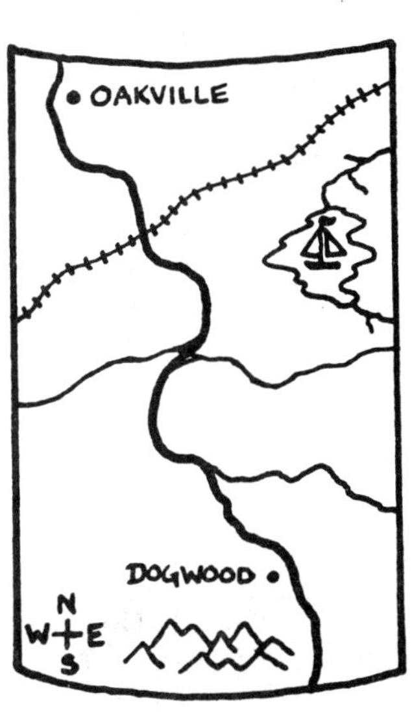
OAKVILLE
DOGWOOD
N
W E
S

a	r	o	u	n	d	m	b	k	j
p	l	u	l	m	h	g	z	s	i
a	q	t	k	d	o	w	n	o	l
h	r	s	j	r	w	d	r	u	o
m	w	i	c	o	t	y	s	t	u
t	x	d	c	r	o	w	d	h	d
r	a	e	h	p	w	w	b	d	l
c	b	g	s	q	n	t	c	e	y
d	c	l	o	u	d	s	w	f	g
m	o	u	n	t	a	i	n	s	h

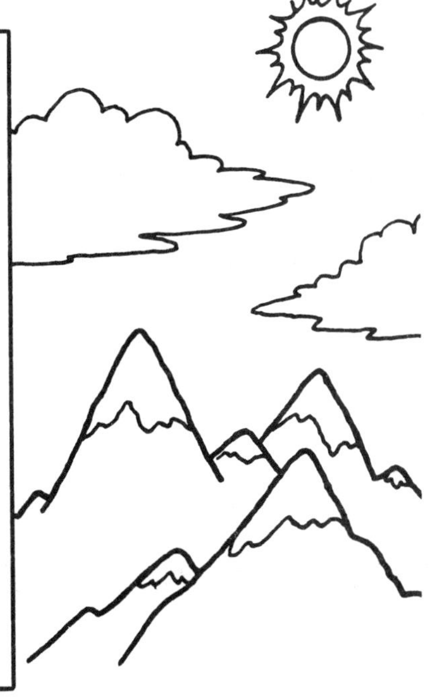

Name ________________________________

Find and circle the word that matches each picture.

spoon
spout
spend

cloud
climb
clown

growl
goose
grease

month
meat
mouth

crow
crawl
crown

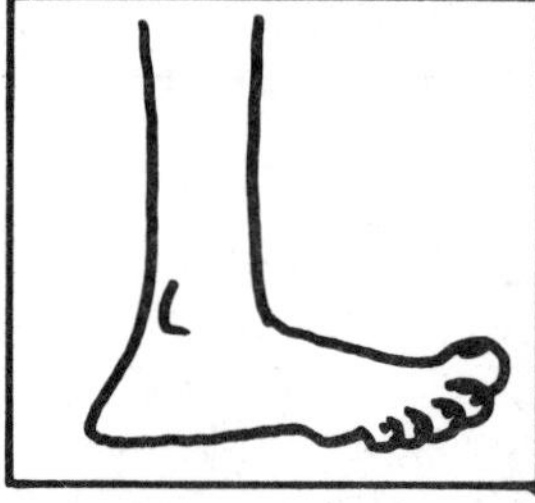

foot
fought
feel

flyer
flower
flavor

FRIES

found
food
feed

mister
moose
mouse

Circle the best answer.

1. something you hear
   send sound soft
2. something in the sky
   main moan moon
3. the name of a color
   brown brand brain
4. A chair is made of ____ .
   wool wood wheat
5. A circle is ____ .
   read round red
6. something to sweep with
   broom blouse brood

Name ______________________________

Write the word that best fits in each sentence below. Cross out the word that does not belong. The picture will give you clues.

1. Jennifer is wearing a ________ .
   crane, crown
2. There is only one ________ in the sky.
   cloud, clown
3. Mark ________ a bone to the dog.
   threw, three
4. Do you think the dog will ________ on the bone?
   chin, chew
5. The sun and the ball are ________ .
   rolled, round
6. Jennifer's ________ has a red ________ on it.
   blush, blouse **flower, floor**
7. The ________ didn't scare our ________ at all.
   mouse, moose **cow, caw**
8. The dog's name is ________ .
   Saw, Sue

Name ______________________________

The vowels **OI** and **OY** make the same sound. Say these words:

coin **boy**

Read each sentence. Write the last three words in the correct order.

1. Please don't make ______________ . much noise so
2. This pencil has ______________ . sharp a point
3. A penny is ______________ . coin a small
4. A good name for a ______________ . Roy boy is
5. Dad said, "I hope you ______________ ." this enjoy toy

Me?!
Yeah, c'mon!
CLUBHOUSE
MEMBERS ONLY
PRIVATE!
GOOD TIRE
RADIAL

Write the word from the list that best completes each sentence.

6. We'd like you to __________ our club.
7. Dad poured a can of __________ in the car.
8. __________ your finger to the answer.
9. Only __________ can leave early.
10. Put the peas in water and let them __________ .

oil
boy
boil
noise
point
Joyce
join

Name ____ Skill: **oy, oi**

Science Experiments

1. All of Mrs. Scott's students ________________ her science class.
2. She lets everyone in her class have the ________________ of which experiment they want to do.
3. Jake decided to do an experiment that smelled like ________________ eggs.
4. Another ________________ named David did an experiment using magnets.
5. Cory and Stacy ________________ together to experiment with electricity.
6. Bill showed the class why ________________ was needed to make a car run smoothly.
7. Lynn's ant farm fell off the table and was ________________.
8. Bob's ________________ volcano erupted and frightened the class.
9. Everyone planted beans in some ________________ to watch them grow.
10. Watching ________________ collect on a glass terrarium was interesting for everyone.

a	n	o	i	n	a	c	m	c	e
j	o	i	n	e	d	h	o	d	e
m	l	k	j	i	b	o	i	f	j
e	n	j	o	y	n	i	s	h	s
n	w	x	i	h	o	c	t	g	p
o	i	l	s	g	i	e	u	k	o
p	v	x	o	f	s	n	r	l	i
q	t	y	i	e	y	b	e	m	l
r	s	c	l	d	c	o	o	p	e
d	e	s	t	r	o	y	e	d	d

Word Box

choice
boy
spoiled
noisy
destroyed
moisture
soil
oil
enjoy
joined

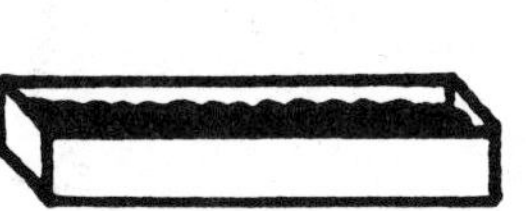

Name ______________________________

AW	AU	OI	OY
draw	caught	coin	boy

Read each sentence. Choose the correct missing word and write it on the line.

1. Most kittens have sharp ______________________ .
   cause claws coil

2. A penny is a ______________________ .
   point coin yawn

3. That car sure makes a lot of ______________________ .
   noise loin lawn

4. My friend's name is ______________________ .
   Paw Toy Roy

5. Put water on the stove and let it ______________________ .
   boil boy blue

6. My dog has one white ______________________ .
   point paw draw

7. This pencil doesn't have a ______________________ .
   auto coil point

8. When I'm tired, I ______________________ .
   join yawn boil

9. I want to buy a new ______________________ .
   jaw toy joy

10. Another word for 'car' is ______________________ .
    bay hawk auto

11. The baby has not learned to ______________________
    crawl claw oil

12. Jim has two sons and one ______________________ .
    voice daughter paw

Name ____________________

EW	UE	OI	OY
new	blue	coin	boy

Circle the words that have the same ending sound as the picture.

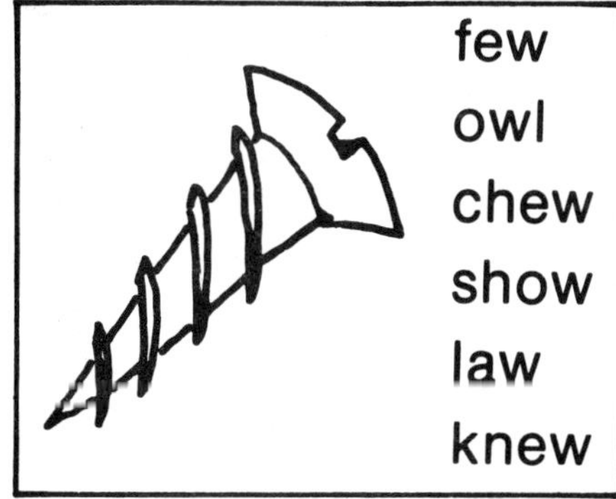

few
owl
chew
show
law
knew

tower
enjoy
boy
house
Roy
threw

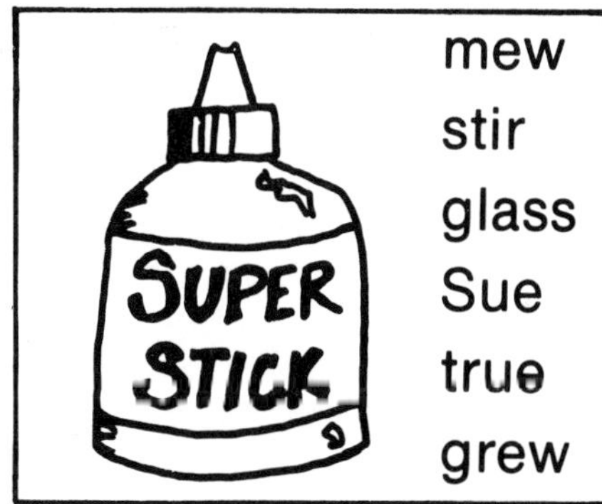
SUPER
STICK

mew
stir
glass
Sue
true
grew

Find the word that best fits in each sentence.

1. I can't __________ this gum.
2. My dad gave me a __________ bike.
3. This line is for girls, not __________ .
4. Plant your seeds in the __________ .
5. I can't guess. Give me a __________ .

choose
clue
claw
sail
boys
soil
bows
noise
new
chew

A vowel sound is missing from one word in each sentence. Choose the correct sound, circle and write it.

6. You're making too much n____se!	ow	oo	oi	ew
7. I'm sure you'll enj____ the play.	ue	ew	ay	oy
8. We need some gl____ to fix this.	aw	ue	us	oi
9. David has four shiny c____ns.	on	ew	oi	ou
10. Anne thr____ the ball to me.	ew	oy	ea	ee

Name ____________________

Read the riddles. Find the best answer and write it on the line.

I'm seen at night.
I'm sometimes round.

What am I? ________

I am a penny.
I am a dime.

I am a ________ .

I am in the circus.
I make people laugh.

Who am I? ________

I am a season.
I am also called "fall."

I am ________ .

A queen wears me.
I'm made of gold.

What am I? ________

Plant a seed in me.
I will help it grow.

What am I? ________

auto
crown
school
boot
screw
owl
autumn
moon
coin
clown
soil
frown

I stay awake at night.
People say I am wise.

What am I? ________

I have wheels.
My other name is "car."

What am I? ________

I am a building.
I have many classrooms.

What am I? ________

I make a sad face,
a bad face, a mad face.

I am a ________ .

I am a kind of shoe.
Cowboys like to wear me.

What am I? ________

I'm made of metal.
I can hold bikes together.

I am a ________ .

RALPH
RABBIT
1 OAK TREE LN.

Name ________________________________

OY	AW	OO	UE	OU
boy	draw	look	blue	house

Write the correct vowel sound for each word.
Use the examples above to help you.

YAA!
m se
c k
sh t
t
I'M A SWELL GUY
SUSAN
h k
b
S
cl
SUPER STICK
h f
gl
cl d
y n

Choose a word from above to complete each sentence.

1. When I'm tired, I __________ .
2. Stick the ends together with __________ .
3. A __________ is a very large bird.
4. I hope you will see __________ at our party.

Name ______________________________

OO AU EW OI OW

Write the word that best completes the sentence. Cross out the incorrect words.

1. This pencil doesn't have a __________ . paint point paste
2. Sue has two sons and one __________ . driver dinner daughter
3. This chair is made of __________ . wood wool wade
4. Another word for 'car' is __________ . auto aunt ought
5. That plant really __________ tall. green grey grew

OY OW OO EU OU

Find the word the matches each picture. Circle it.

6. 

clue
clam
claw
clay

7. 

moon
mane
mine
moan

8. 

bloom
blast
blouse
blow

9. 

jam
jaw
jar
jay

10. 
SUSAN

Sue
saw
say
sow

11. 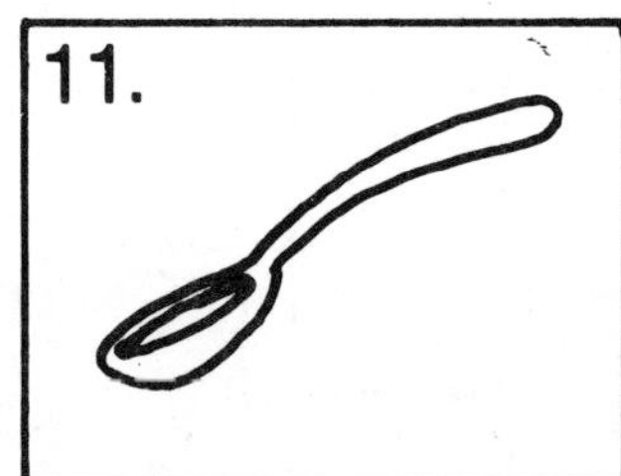

spin
spool
soon
spoon

Write the word from the list that best completes each sentence.

12. The month after July is __________ .
13. Would you like to swim in our __________?
14. A penny is a small __________ .
15. Please! Don't __________ in my ear!
16. Always __________ your meat well.

pool	cone
chew	shout
shut	pail
Autumn	coin
chin	August

Name ______________________________ Skill: **ea, ee, ei, ie**

Rainy Day Fun

Word Box
weave
eight
see
piece
dream
need
cheese
easy
sheets
believable

1. On rainy days you only ______________ to use your imagination to think of fun things to do.
2. Draw pictures using some ______________ of colored paper and crayons.
3. Make a grilled ______________ sandwich for lunch.
4. ______________ about going to faraway places.
5. ______________ a place mat using strips of paper.
6. Write a ______________ story about a trip you once took.
7. Eat a ______________ of carrot cake as you wait for the sun to shine again.
8. List ______________ things to do when the weather clears.
9. ______________ how many words you can make out of the word **sunshine**.
10. It's ______________ to have fun when you use your imagination!

s	e	v	w	a	n	n	t	e	d
h	c	h	e	e	s	e	i	d	r
e	e	r	a	a	k	e	e	c	e
e	y	t	v	s	n	d	b	a	a
t	h	i	e	y	o	h	e	u	m
s	n	g	w	p	w	a	v	s	i
v	i	h	e	i	g	h	t	e	w
e	s	a	e	e	e	h	t	n	o
e	e	v	r	c	l	o	c	a	l
b	e	l	i	e	v	a	b	l	e

Name ________________________________ Skill: **ci, si, ti**

The Surprise Party

Welcome Home Gail!

Word Box
occasion
suspicious
musician
directions
patient
invitation
special
mission
permission
mention

p	e	r	m	i	s	s	i	o	n
s	u	s	p	i	c	i	o	u	s
m	o	p	a	t	i	e	n	t	p
m	u	s	i	c	i	a	n	h	e
p	m	e	n	t	i	o	n	j	c
k	e	m	i	s	s	i	o	n	i
l	o	c	c	a	s	i	o	n	a
b	t	s	n	r	c	o	a	w	l
i	n	v	i	t	a	t	i	o	n
d	i	r	e	c	t	i	o	n	s

1. Sandy had to write one more ____________________ for Gail's surprise party.
2. She put a map with ____________________ to Gail's house in the envelope and she was finished.
3. This was to be a very ____________________ party.
4. Gail had been a ____________________ in the hospital for many weeks and now she was coming home.
5. Sandy had told everyone not to ____________________ the party to Gail.
6. A ____________________ had been hired to play.
7. Gail's mother had given Gail's friends ____________________ to give her a kitten as a welcome-home gift.
8. Gail wasn't at all ____________________ as she opened the door.
9. The ____________________ to keep the party a surprise had succeeded.
10. This was a happy ____________________ for Gail and everyone.

Name ________________________________ Skill: **squ, qu**

The Aquarium

1. Mother agreed to let Jim and Susan have an aquarium because fish are ______________.
2. Jim went to the pet store and asked many ______________ about starting an aquarium.
3. He found out that an aquarium holds many ______________ of water.
4. He bought a ______________ shaped aquarium and took it home.
5. He and Susan began to ______________ about what kind of fish to keep in it.
6. Finally, Susan took six of her own ______________ to buy the fish she wanted.
7. She carried the fish home carefully so she didn't ______________ it.
8. The fish ______________ around unhappily in its tiny container.
9. Susan ______________ with delight as she put the fish in the aquarium.
10. She laughed when her fish ______________ Jim with water.

q	u	q	u	a	r	r	e	l	s
u	u	e	u	s	t	d	s	a	q
e	s	a	n	g	z	l	q	x	u
s	q	i	r	m	k	e	u	q	i
t	u	o	r	t	o	a	e	u	r
i	a	y	e	e	s	n	a	i	m
o	s	q	u	a	r	e	l	e	e
n	h	x	a	i	c	n	e	t	d
s	q	u	i	r	t	e	d	e	e
n	s	q	u	a	r	t	e	r	s

Word Box
quarts
questions
quarrel
quiet
square
squash
squealed
squirmed
quarters
squirted

Name ______________________________ Skill: Silent consonants

My New Pet

Word Box
- trick
- comb
- Fluffy
- patch
- whole
- glistens
- whistle
- know
- stretch
- climbing

g	s	t	r	e	t	c	h	c	w
F	l	r	p	t	s	o	d	l	h
l	s	i	o	p	u	m	o	i	i
u	p	c	s	a	v	b	b	m	s
f	e	k	n	t	w	x	a	b	t
f	c	q	m	c	e	y	y	i	l
y	i	r	l	h	z	n	x	n	e
l	a	k	n	o	w	e	s	g	u
x	z	r	t	l	m	n	w	v	t
o	p	o	w	h	o	l	e	r	s

1. I have a new pet that I ______________ you would like to have.
2. His name is ______________ because he has such soft fur.
3. I brush and ______________ his fur every day.
4. I brush his coat so much that his fur ______________.
5. He loves to ______________ out on the floor at the foot of my bed at night.
6. Fluffy wakes me up in the morning by ______________ up on my bed.
7. He is all black with a ______________ of white over one eye.
8. When I ______________ for Fluffy, he comes running right to me.
9. The ______________ Fluffy does best is "shaking hands."
10. I'm the luckiest boy in the ______________ world to have a puppy like Fluffy.

Name ____ Skill: 3-letter blends

Spring Things

1. When ____________________ arrives there are always so many things to do.
2. At our house, we ____________________ up the work so that we can get it done faster.
3. I pick up any ____________________ paper that has blown onto the lawn.
4. Dad ____________________ the lawn to keep it green.
5. ____________________ unwanted weeds begin to grow in the grass.
6. Dad has to ____________________ them to get rid of them.
7. Mother trims all of the ____________________ around the yard.
8. My brother Mark is so ____________________, he carries the patio furniture out of the garage and puts it on the patio.
9. Sometimes I polish the ____________________ on Mom's car.
10. All of these activities remind me that I'll be out of ____________________ for summer vacation soon.

Word Box

strange
chrome
split
school
sprinkles
scrap
strong
spring
spray
shrubs

s	h	s	c	t	r	a	c	s	c
s	s	c	h	o	o	l	r	t	h
s	p	r	r	r	n	y	s	r	r
h	r	a	s	p	l	i	t	o	o
r	i	p	t	j	n	o	k	n	m
u	n	l	s	t	r	a	n	g	e
b	k	t	u	s	p	r	a	y	o
s	l	b	a	s	p	r	i	n	g
a	e	m	s	g	f	x	t	n	a
c	s	r	l	s	n	o	b	y	t

Name ______________________ Skill: hard **c**, soft **c**

The Best Birthday Party

Word Box
- come
- computer
- ice
- danced
- cotton
- excited
- clown
- magic
- cake
- became

c	l	d	g	a	e	m	a	c	d
o	l	c	r	e	x	n	n	o	a
t	s	o	b	i	c	e	c	m	n
t	t	m	w	h	i	g	a	p	c
o	h	e	u	n	t	o	k	u	e
n	e	m	n	l	e	f	e	t	d
e	l	a	i	q	d	o	n	e	e
r	n	g	m	g	m	o	e	r	s
i	s	i	o	j	e	i	r	c	u
b	e	c	a	m	e	n	b	e	a

1. Tom was very ______________ about his birthday party.
2. He couldn't wait to see the ______________ show his mother had planned.
3. His friend Carol arrived first; then the others began to ______________.
4. A ______________ began to make everyone laugh.
5. He ______________ around the room.
6. Tom gave everyone some ______________ candy to eat.
7. Then they all had birthday ______________ and ice cream.
8. Tom got a pair of ______________ skates from his friend Sam.
9. His mother and dad gave him a ______________.
10. This birthday ______________ the very best birthday Tom had ever had.

Name ______________________________ Skill: hard **g**, soft **g**

The Scavenger Hunt

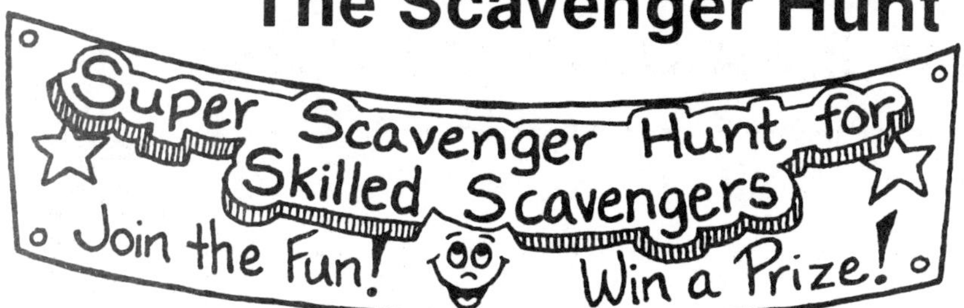
Super Scavenger Hunt for
Skilled Scavengers
Join the Fun!
Win a Prize!

Word Box
goose
giraffe
scavenger
magazine
green
going
wig
marriage
challenge
postage

1. My friend Amy and I like ____________ on scavenger hunts.
2. It's a good thing Amy and I enjoy a ____________ like that, because it can be difficult to find all of the items.
3. The easiest thing to collect is ____________ leaves.
4. A ____________ feather was one of the most difficult things to find.
5. We went to a pet shop to find the feather and we also got a picture of a tall ____________ there.
6. My uncle had the blue clown's ____________ we needed.
7. Amy's mother gave us a ____________ stamp.
8. A neighbor gave us a ____________ dated two years ago.
9. My mom gave us the last item we needed—a ____________ license.
10. To our surprise, Amy and I won the ____________ hunt and got a blue ribbon.

g	m	a	g	a	z	i	n	e	c
s	a	g	i	r	a	f	f	e	h
c	r	r	g	i	r	t	m	c	a
a	r	e	e	c	h	r	p	z	l
v	i	e	a	n	i	s	o	b	l
e	a	n	o	w	i	g	s	r	e
n	g	r	r	g	e	o	t	y	n
g	e	b	h	o	s	i	a	f	g
e	g	o	o	s	e	n	g	x	e
r	c	a	v	e	t	g	e	r	a

FIRST
PRIZE!
BEST
SCAVENGER
HUNTER

Name ______________________________

Read the words in the Word Box.
Write the word that completes each sentence.
Circle the words in the puzzle.

1. Paul asked Dad to read him a ________________.
2. It is ________________ when the sun shines.
3. Mary will ________________ to win the race.
4. Jon was ________________ to get a new puppy.
5. The new girl in school was very ________________.
6. My big brother, Joe, is ________________ years old.
7. ________________ can't we go to the zoo today?
8. The ________________ is blue today.

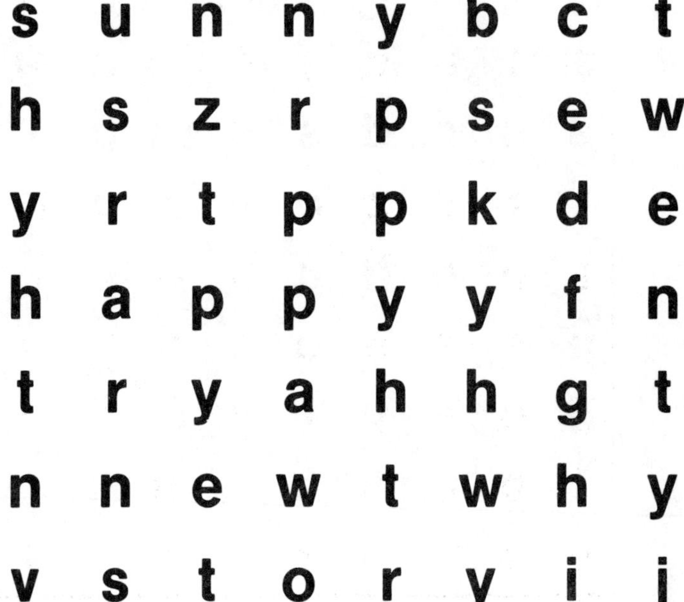

s	u	n	n	y	b	c	t
h	s	z	r	p	s	e	w
y	r	t	p	p	k	d	e
h	a	p	p	y	y	f	n
t	r	y	a	h	h	g	t
n	n	e	w	t	w	h	y
v	s	t	o	r	y	i	j

Word Box

- story
- try
- shy
- why
- sunny
- happy
- sky
- twenty

Name ______________________________ Skill: Vowel sound of **y**

Camping Fun

1. Joey and Pete go camping ____________ Lake Carter with their family.
2. It makes both boys very ______________________ to go camping.
3. They are always very ______________________ every day at camp.
4. The boys like to ______________________ nature and collect things.
5. Pete's ______________________ is collecting wild flowers.
6. ______________________ enjoys cooking over a camp fire.
7. The boys were so excited when they saw a hive of ______________________ bees on their last trip.
8. It is even more fun than usual when Pete's dog ______________________ goes along.
9. Joey and Pete __________________ to get their family to go on at least three camping trips each summer.
10. If the boys want to write a ______________________ for school about their summer vacation, they will have more than enough adventures to write about.

i	l	b	e	r	o	t	h	o	v
s	t	u	d	y	h	y	a	m	s
a	n	s	d	s	u	m	p	i	t
t	r	y	z	o	u	s	p	h	o
z	n	n	h	o	n	e	y	L	r
p	e	r	h	o	b	b	y	u	y
J	o	e	y	t	y	i	c	c	t
t	n	a	t	b	x	m	u	k	t
y	m	n	i	r	s	t	l	y	r

Word Box
- study
- Joey
- busy
- try
- story
- Lucky
- honey
- hobby
- happy
- by

Name ____________________ Skill: **—ed** sound

Jamie's Bedroom

Word Box
- selected
- looked
- wasted
- stopped
- asked
- filled
- placed
- hummed
- grinned
- repaired

l	o	l	b	i	g	n	s	e	h
w	o	d	e	f	a	i	e	l	u
a	u	o	i	i	s	r	l	e	m
s	f	p	k	m	k	e	e	s	m
t	i	l	n	e	e	p	c	t	e
e	l	a	a	a	d	a	t	o	d
d	l	c	r	j	o	i	e	p	e
i	e	e	e	l	t	r	d	p	s
c	d	d	a	m	r	e	v	e	t
g	r	i	n	n	e	d	n	d	s

1. Jamie ____________________ no time at all before moving his things into his new bedroom.
2. He ____________________ all of his sweaters on hangers and put them in the closet.
3. He ____________________ working to plan where the rest of his furniture would go.
4. Then Jamie ____________________ his shelves with books and model planes.
5. He ____________________ a favorite baseball poster to hang on the wall.
6. He ____________________ his mom if he could keep his computer in his room.
7. Jamie ____________________ his favorite song as he worked.
8. He was surprised how great his room ____________________.
9. He was so glad his dad had ____________________ the broken window.
10. Jamie ____________________ from ear to ear as he looked around his wonderful bedroom.

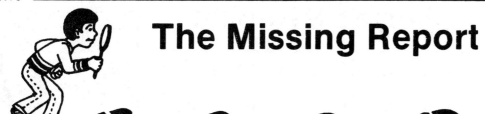

Name ______________________________ Skill: **—ed, —ing**

The Missing Report

REPORT

1. As I ______________ to go into my classroom, I checked to see if I had my report, but I couldn't find it.
2. I had spent two hours ______________ on that report the night before.
3. Mr. Chapman, my teacher, ______________ me at the door.
4. I knew he wouldn't be ______________ that I couldn't find my report.
5. ______________ until Mr. Chapman asked for the reports was torture.
6. Finally he said, "The reports can now be ______________ to the front of the room."
7. Mr. Chapman saw that my paper was ______________.
8. He ______________ me to look for it in my desk and backpack.
9. How ______________ I was to find it in my backpack!
10. I ______________ no time handing in my report.

w	a	s	t	e	d	v	w	s	s
r	s	t	t	u	p	g	o	t	u
s	k	a	v	w	a	r	r	u	r
d	e	r	x	y	s	e	k	m	p
e	d	t	l	z	s	e	i	i	r
p	l	e	m	f	e	t	n	s	i
b	a	d	n	g	d	e	g	s	s
p	l	e	a	s	e	d	o	i	e
o	j	i	h	k	l	n	p	n	d
w	a	i	t	i	n	g	q	g	r

Word Box
missing
surprised
waiting
greeted
started
working
passed
wasted
asked
pleased

Name ______________________________ Skill: **—er, —est**

My Best Friend

1. I have many nice friends, but Pat is my ____________ friend.
2. Just talking to Pat when I'm sad makes me feel ____________.
3. She is ____________ than my other friends because she is so thoughtful.
4. Pat always makes me laugh because she tells the ____________ jokes.
5. We are both good ____________ and members of the swim team.
6. Pat is about a head ____________ than I am.
7. She can do many things ____________ than I can.
8. I tell Pat all my secrets because she is a good ____________ and I can trust her.
9. I have known Pat ____________ than any friend.
10. Have you guessed by now that Pat is my ____________ sister?

o	t	a	l	l	e	r	s	s	f
l	n	i	n	g	a	v	e	w	u
d	h	a	p	p	i	e	r	i	n
e	n	e	i	i	h	w	n	m	n
r	l	o	n	g	e	r	b	m	i
f	u	s	h	j	s	m	e	e	e
k	i	n	d	e	r	i	t	r	s
t	e	t	t	u	m	p	t	s	t
h	n	i	c	e	s	t	e	n	g
l	i	s	t	e	n	e	r	o	v

Word Box
- happier
- taller
- better
- older
- nicest
- kinder
- swimmers
- listener
- funniest
- longer

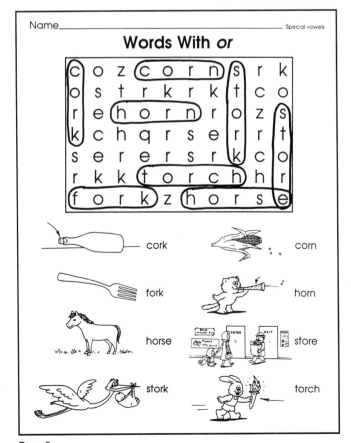

Answer Key

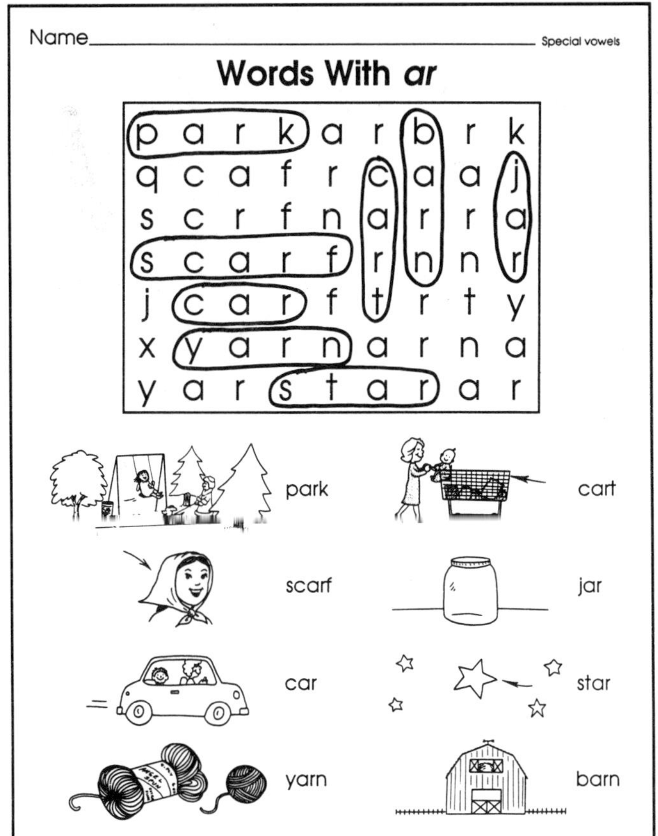

Name________________________ Special vowels

Words With *ar*

p	a	r	k	a	r	b	r	k
q	c	a	f	r	c	a	a	j
s	c	r	f	n	a	r	r	a
s	c	a	r	f	r	n	n	r
j	c	a	r	f	t	r	t	y
x	y	a	r	n	a	r	n	a
y	a	r	s	t	a	r	a	r

park cart scarf jar car star yarn barn

Page 1

Name________________________ Special vowels

Words With *ar*

							1 b	
							a	
					2 c	a	r	d
					a		n	
		3 s	c	4 a	r	f		
		t		r				
		a		m				
5 c	a	r	t					

Word Box
star
arm
car
cart
scarf
card
barn

Across

2. 3. 5.

Down

1. 2. 3. 4.

Page 2

Name________________________ Special vowels

Words With *or*

c	o	z	c	o	r	n	s	r	k
o	s	t	r	k	r	k	t	c	o
r	e	h	o	r	n	r	o	z	s
k	c	h	q	r	s	e	r	r	t
s	e	r	e	r	s	r	k	c	o
r	k	k	t	o	r	c	h	h	r
f	o	r	k	z	h	o	r	s	e

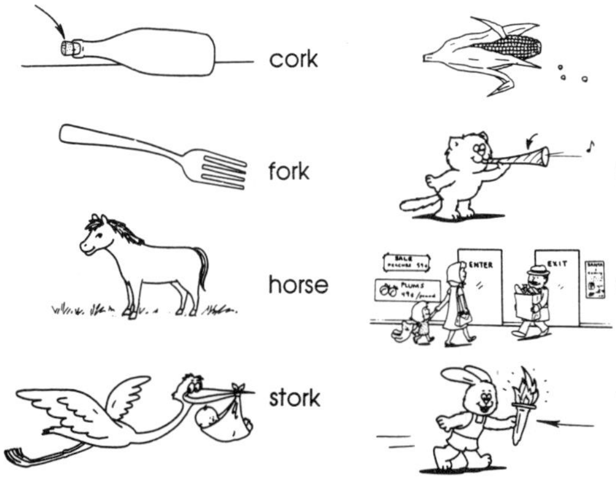

cork corn fork horn horse store stork torch

Page 3

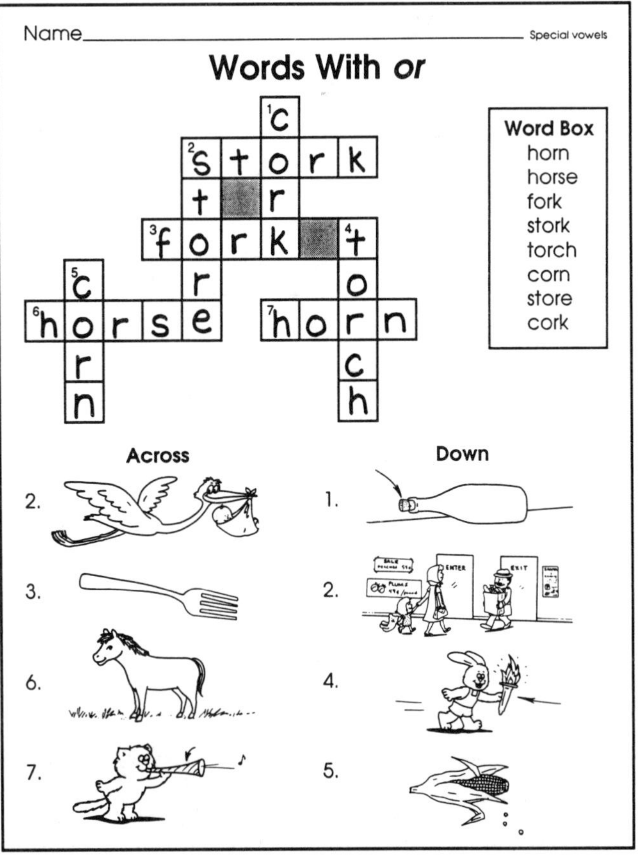

Name________________________ Special vowels

Words With *or*

						1 c			
				2 s	t	o	r	k	
				t		r			
			3 f	o	r	k		4 t	
	5 c			r				o	
6 h	o	r	s	e		7 h	o	r	n
	r							c	
	n							h	

Word Box
horn
horse
fork
stork
torch
corn
store
cork

Across

2. 3. 6. 7.

Down

1. 2. 4. 5.

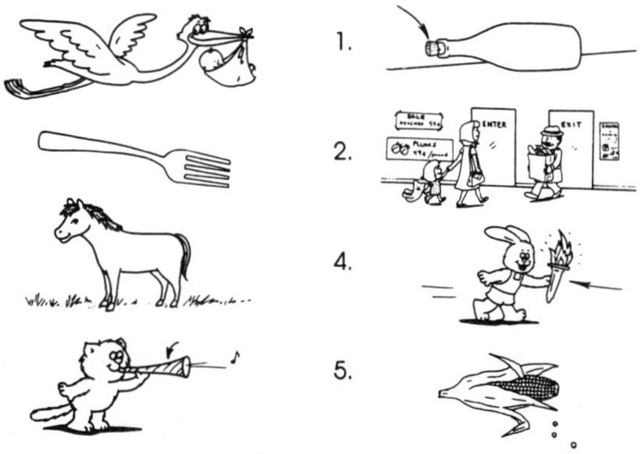

Page 4

Answer Key

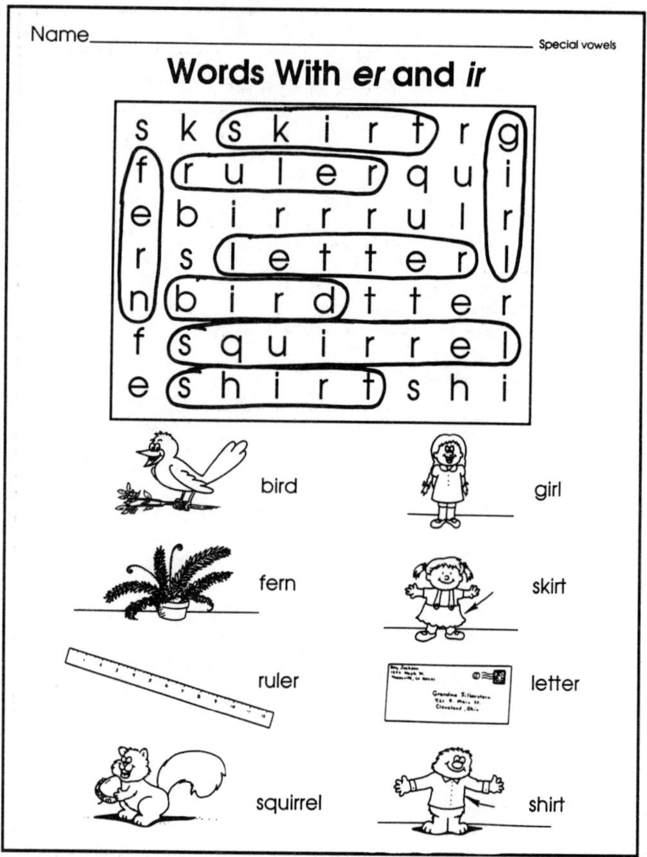

Name______________________ Special vowels

Words With *er* and *ir*

s	k	s	k	i	r	t	r	g
f	r	u	l	e	r	q	u	i
e	b	i	r	r	r	u	l	r
r	s	l	e	t	t	e	r	l
n	b	i	r	d	t	t	e	r
f	s	q	u	i	r	r	e	l
e	s	h	i	r	t	s	h	i

bird girl
fern skirt
ruler letter
squirrel shirt

Page 5

Name______________________ Special vowels

Words With *er* and *ir*

Word Box
fern
girl
letter
ruler
shirt
skirt
squirrel

1 skirt
1 squirrel
2 shirt
3 ruler
4 fern
5 girl
6 letter

Across

1.

4.

5.

6.

Down

1.

2.

3.

Page 6

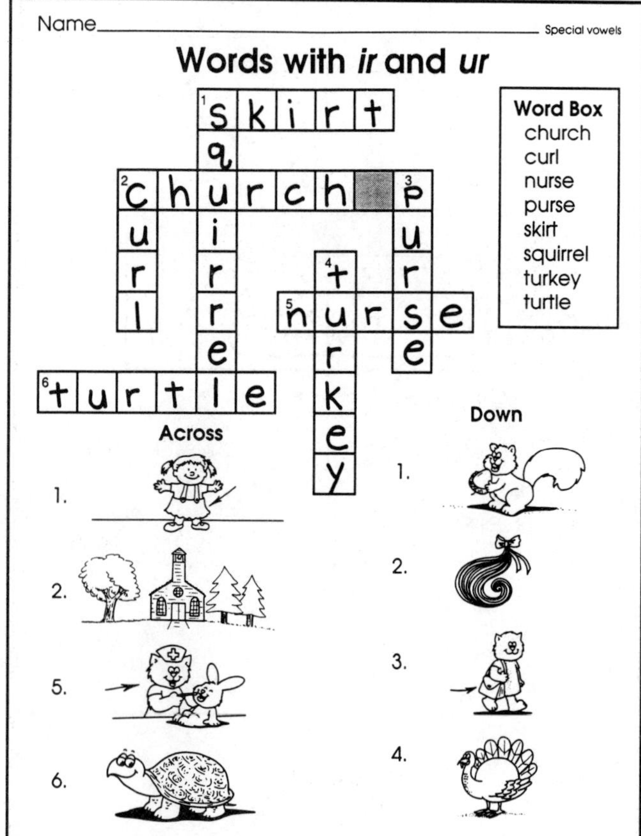

Name______________________ Special vowels

Words with *ir* and *ur*

Word Box
church
curl
nurse
purse
skirt
squirrel
turkey
turtle

1 skirt
1 squirrel
2 church
2 curl
3 purse
4 turkey
5 nurse
6 turtle

Across

1.

2.

5.

6.

Down

1.

2.

3.

4.

Page 7

Name______________________ Special vowels

Words With *ea* and *ey*

m	o	n	k	e	y	k	e	b	t
h	s	w	e	a	t	e	r	r	h
h	s	w	k	e	y	n	k	e	r
e	y	n	k	m	n	e	y	a	e
a	f	e	a	t	h	e	r	d	a
d	c	h	i	m	n	e	y	y	d

monkey sweater
head key
feather chimney
bread thread

Page 8

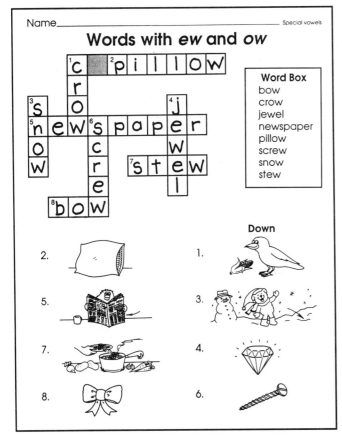

Answer Key

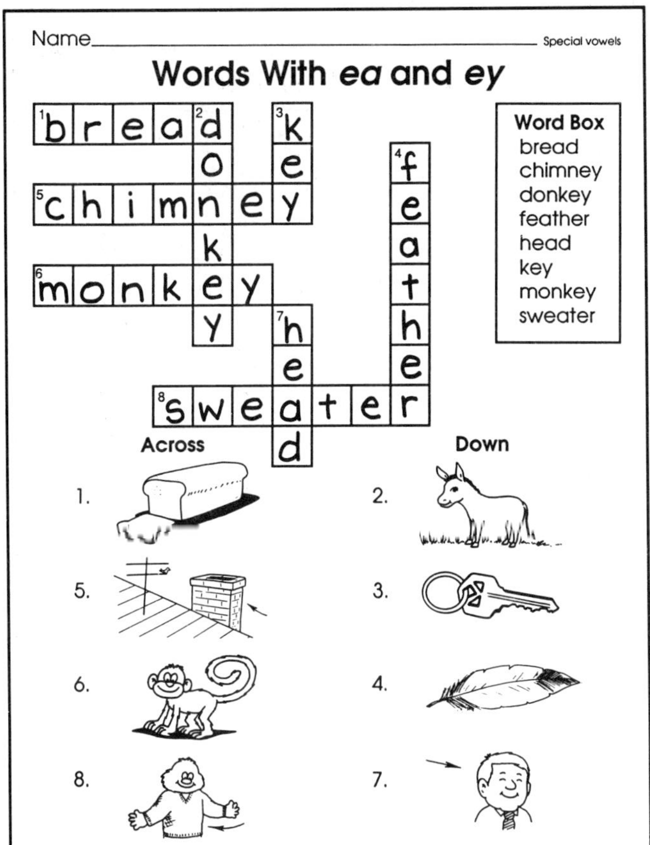

Name______________________________ Special vowels

Words With *ea* and *ey*

1 b	r	e	a	2 d		3 k			
				o		e			4 f
5 c	h	i	m	n	e	y			e
				k					a
6 m	o	n	k	e	y				t
				y		7 h			h
						e			e
			8 s	w	e	a	t	e	r
						d			

Word Box
bread
chimney
donkey
feather
head
key
monkey
sweater

Across — Down

1.
2.
5.
3.
6.
4.
8.
7.

Page 9

Name______________________________ Special vowels

Words With *ew* and *ow*

w w i n d o w j s
i w m n d l l s c
b p i l l o w t r
o j e s n s n e e
w j e w e l r w w
l s c r o w p i l
s n o w m a n j e

jewel
crow
window
pillow
bowl
snowman
stew
screw

Page 10

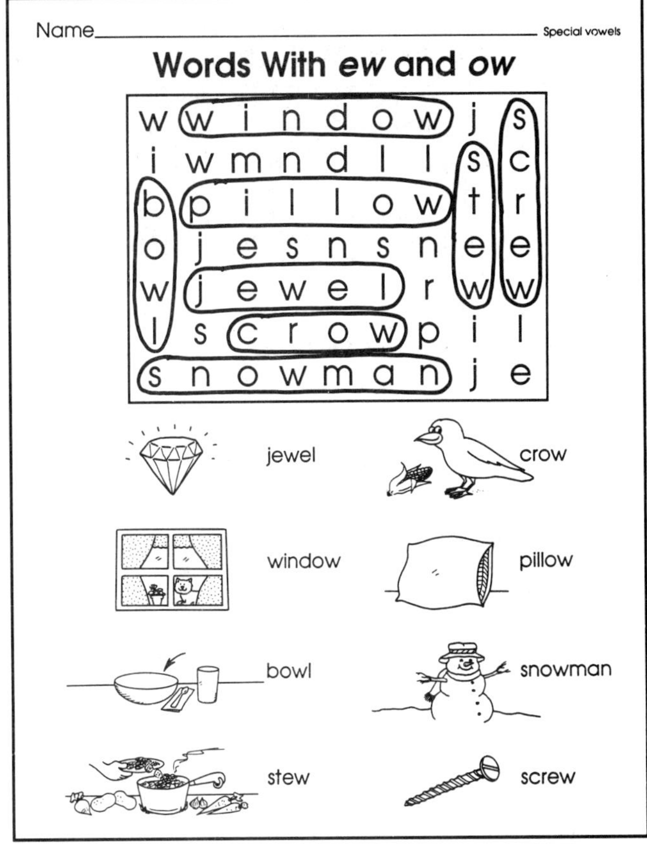

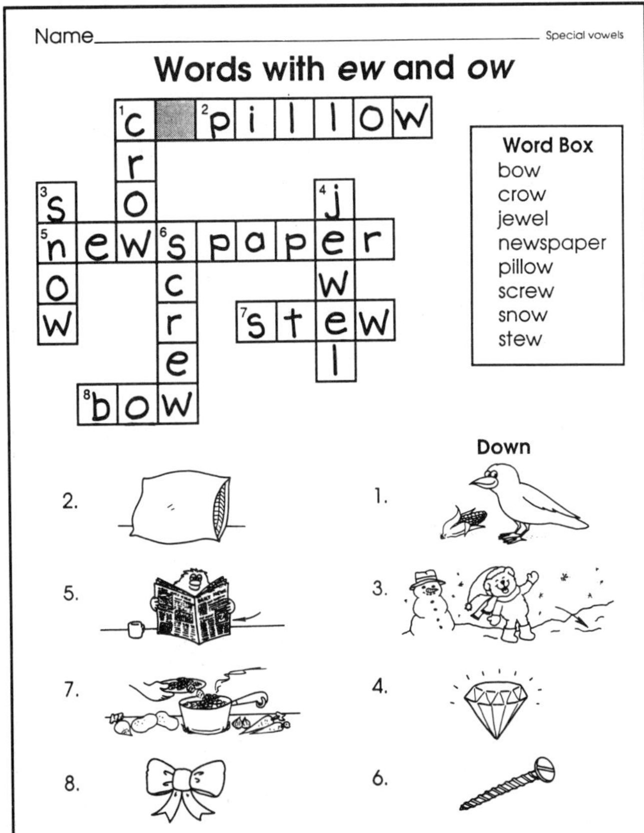

Name______________________________ Special vowels

Words with *ew* and *ow*

		1 c	■	2 p	i	l	l	o	w
		r							
3 s		o					4 j		
5 n	e	w	6 s	p	a	p	e	r	
o			c				w		
w			r		7 s	t	e	w	
			e				l		
	8 b	o	w						

Word Box
bow
crow
jewel
newspaper
pillow
screw
snow
stew

Down

2.
1.
5.
3.
7.
4.
8.
6.

Page 11

Name______________________________ Special vowels

Words With *ow*

c l c l o w n w n
r g o w n l w n e
o f l n t o w e l
w w o w l q q x w
d w n c r o w n n
d f l o w e r e l

clown
gown
towel
flower
owl
crown
crowd

Page 12

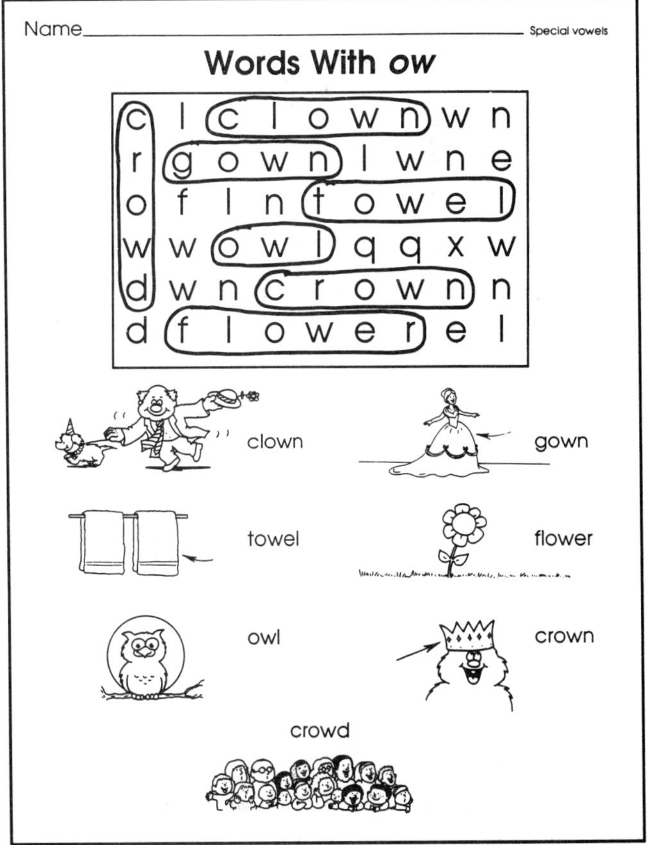

Answer Key

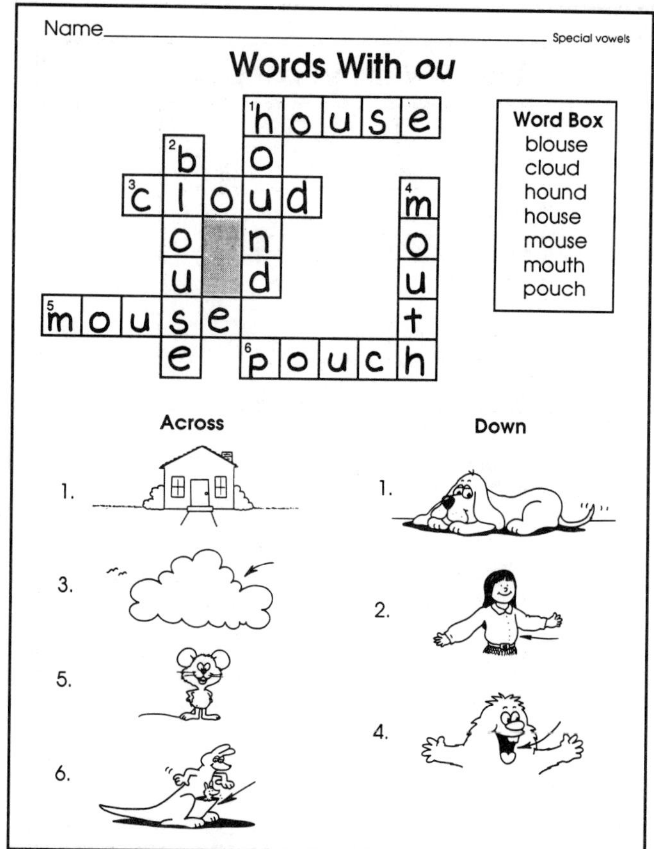

Name________________ Special vowels

Words With *ou*

Word Box
blouse
cloud
hound
house
mouse
mouth
pouch

Across: 1. house 3. cloud 5. mouse 6. pouch

Down: 1. hound 2. blouse 4. mouth

Page 13

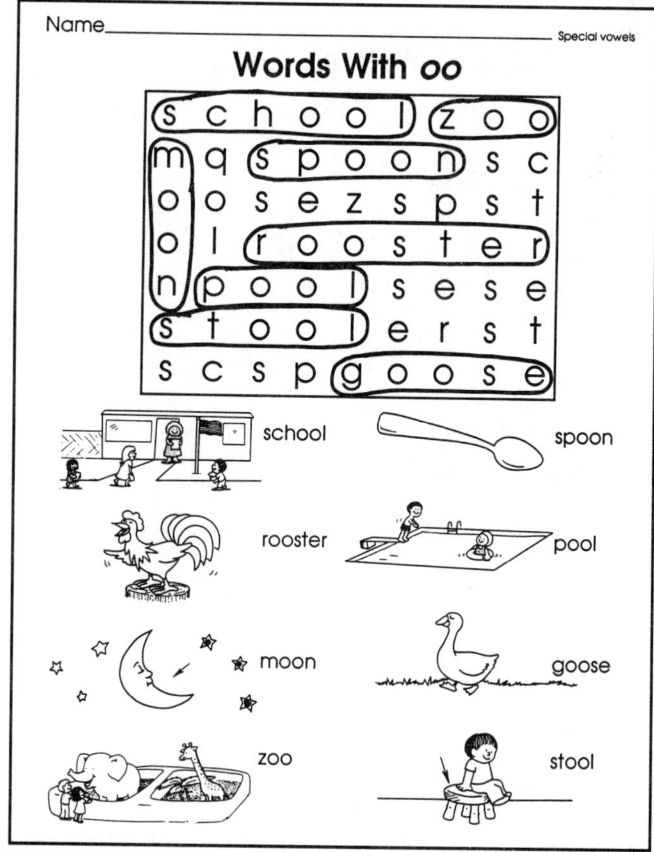

Name________________ Special vowels

Words With *oo*

s	c	h	o	o	l	z	o	o
m	q	s	p	o	o	n	s	c
o	o	s	e	z	s	p	s	t
o	l	r	o	o	s	t	e	r
n	p	o	o	l	s	e	s	e
s	t	o	o	l	e	r	s	t
s	c	s	p	g	o	o	s	e

school, spoon, rooster, pool, moon, goose, zoo, stool

Page 14

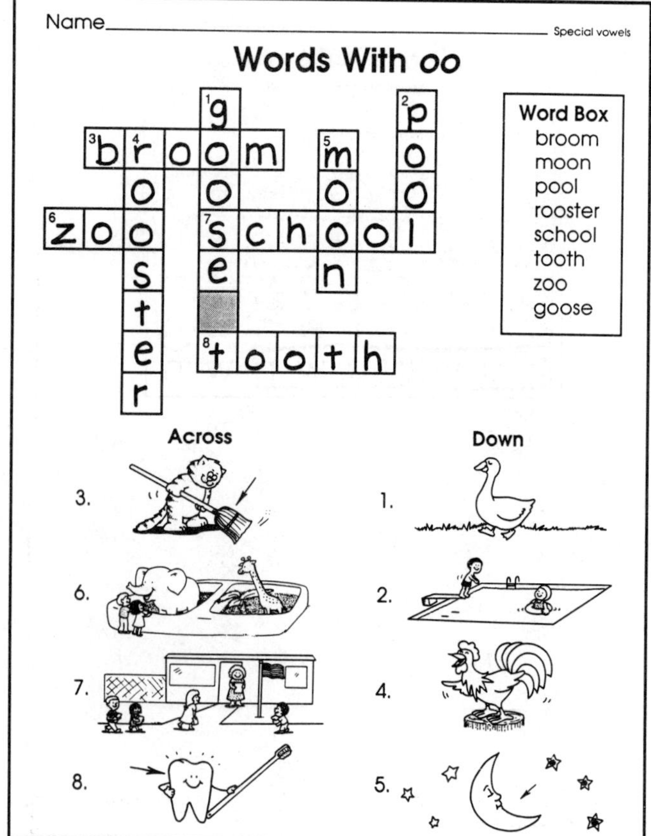

Name________________ Special vowels

Words With *oo*

Word Box
broom
moon
pool
rooster
school
tooth
zoo
goose

Across: 3. broom 6. zoo 7. school 8. tooth

Down: 1. goose 2. pool 4. rooster 5. moon

Page 15

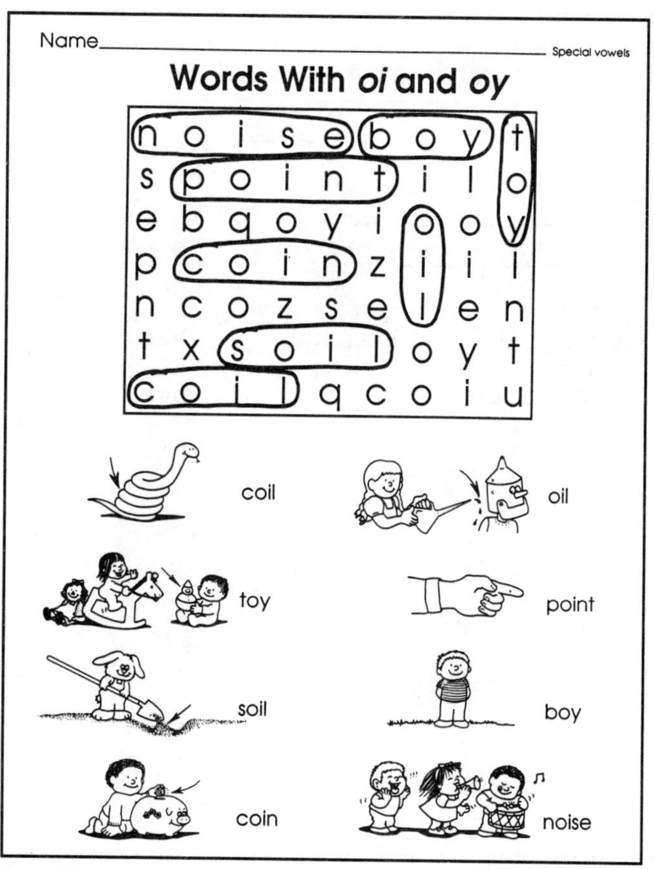

Name________________ Special vowels

Words With *oi* and *oy*

n	o	i	s	e	b	o	y	t
s	p	o	i	n	t	i	l	o
e	b	q	o	y	i	o	o	y
p	c	o	i	n	z	i	i	l
n	c	o	z	s	e	l	e	n
t	x	s	o	i	l	o	y	t
c	o	i	l	q	c	o	i	u

coil, oil, toy, point, soil, boy, coin, noise

Page 16

Answer Key

Name______ Special vowels

Words With *oi* and *oy*

								[1] c	
	[2] b						[3] t	o	y
[4] n	o	i	[5] s	e		[6] c		i	
	y		o		[7] p	o	i	n	t
		[8] o	i	l		i			
			l			l			

Word Box
boy
coil
coin
noise
point
oil
soil
toy

Across
3.
4.
7.
8.

Down
1.
2.
5.
6.

Page 17

Name______ Special vowels

Words With *oo* and *oy*

b	o	o	k	o	v	o	o	k
o	d	b	k	o	c	o	o	k
q	h	o	o	d	w	o	d	h
x	o	o	o	b	k	b	x	o
w	o	o	d	c	k	o	o	o
w	o	m	t	o	y	y	y	k
f	o	o	t	c	o	q	o	t

wood
boy
toy
book
hood
cook
hook
foot

Page 18

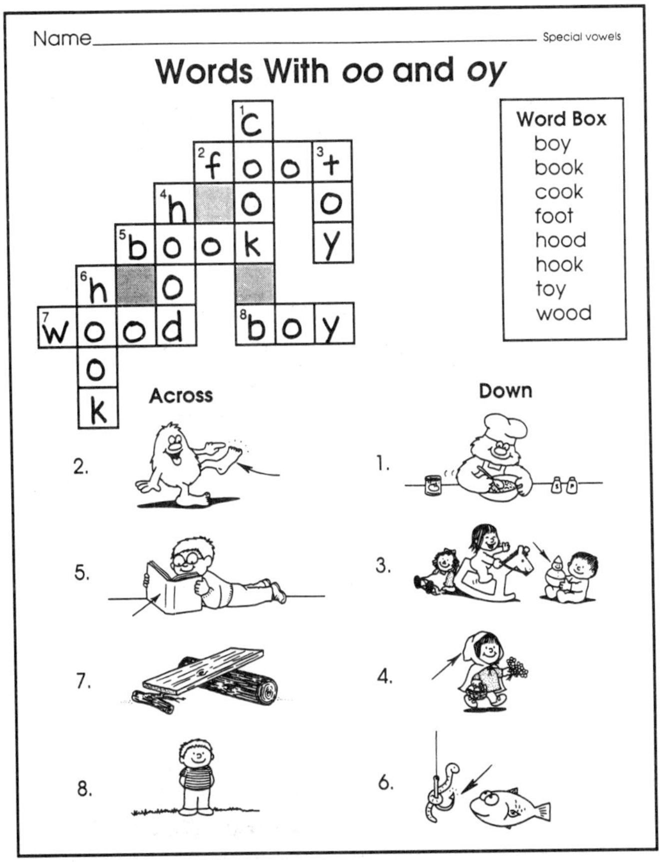
Name______ Special vowels

Words With *oo* and *oy*

					[1] c		
				[2] f	o	o	[3] t
			[4] h		o		o
		[5] b	o	o	k		y
	[6] h		o				
[7] w	o	o	d		[8] b	o	y
	o						
	k						

Word Box
boy
book
cook
foot
hood
hook
toy
wood

Across
2.
5.
7.
8.

Down
1.
3.
4.
6.

Page 19

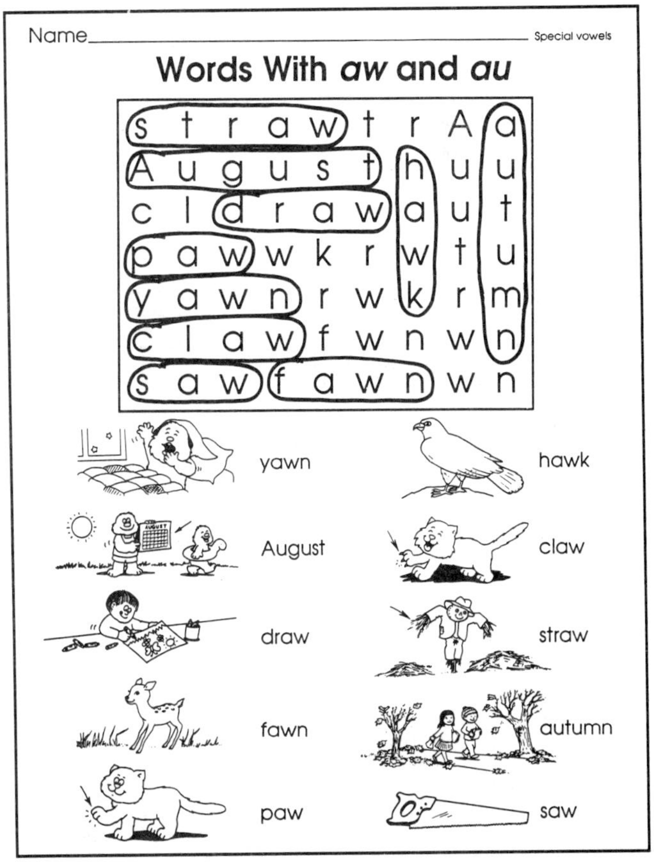
Name______ Special vowels

Words With *aw* and *au*

s	t	r	a	w	t	r	A	a
A	u	g	u	s	t	h	u	u
c	l	d	r	a	w	a	u	t
p	a	w	w	k	r	w	t	u
y	a	w	n	r	w	k	r	m
c	l	a	w	f	w	n	w	n
s	a	w	f	a	w	n	w	n

yawn
hawk
August
claw
draw
straw
fawn
autumn
paw
saw

Page 20

Answer Key

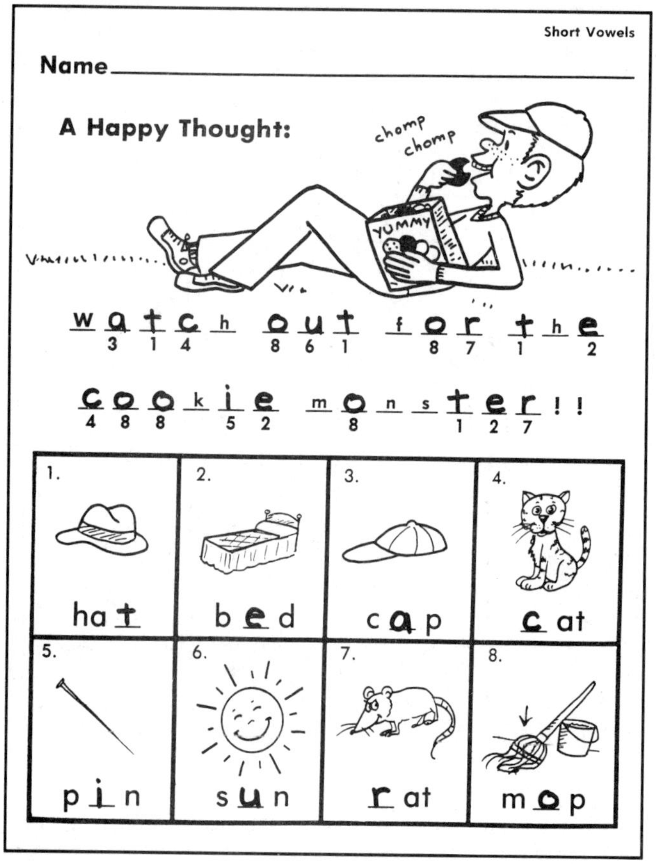

Short Vowels

Name ____________

A Happy Thought:

chomp chomp
YUMMY

watch out for the cookie monster!!

(3 1 4 — 8 6 1 — 8 7 — 1 2 — 4 8 8 5 2 — 8 — 1 2 7)

1. hat	2. bed	3. cap	4. cat
5. pin	6. sun	7. rat	8. mop

Page 21

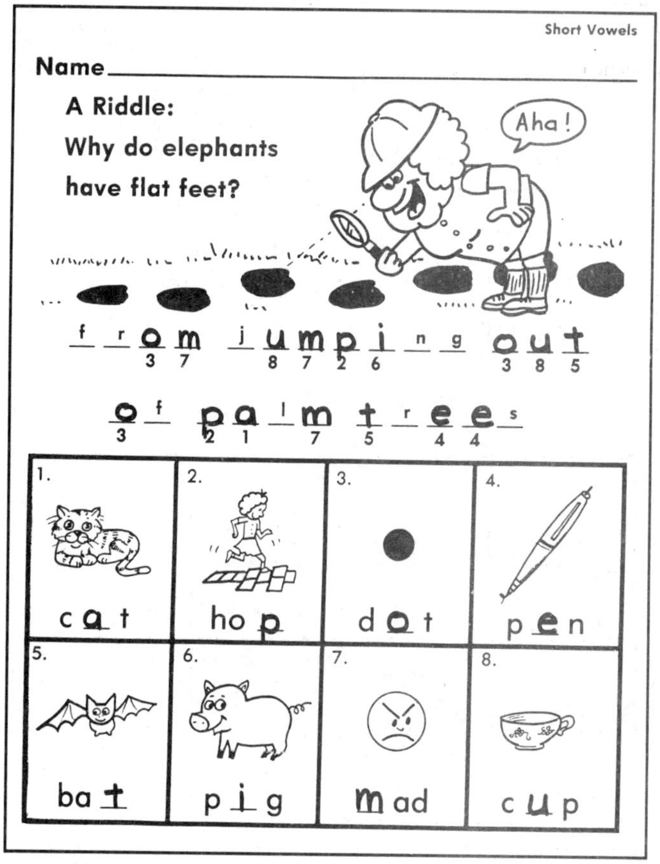

Short Vowels

Name ____________

A Riddle:
Why do elephants have flat feet?

Aha!

from jumping out of palm trees

(3 7 — 8 7 2 6 — 3 8 5 — 3 — 2 1 7 — 5 4 4)

1. cat	2. hop	3. dot	4. pen
5. bat	6. pig	7. mad	8. cup

Page 22

Short Vowels

Name ____________

A Riddle:
At what table do you never sit to eat?

Well, I'll eat anywhere!

multiplication table

(5 7 2 6 7 6 3 2 6 8 — 2 3 4 7 1)

1. hen	2. net	3. pan	4. tub
5. rug	6. wig	7. lip	8. log

Page 23

Short Vowels

Name ____________

A Tongue Twister:

Ho ho
Aha ha!
tee hee

Five fat funny fellows feel fine.

(6 8 2 — 6 4 — 6 7 1 1 — 6 2 3 3 5 — 6 2 2 3 — 6 8 1 2)

1. men	2. ten	3. lock	4. can
5. jog	6. fan	7. jug	8. pig

Page 24

Answer Key

Short Vowels
Name
A Riddle:
How many sides does a coconut have?
two inside and outside
1. mop
2. nest
3. bug
4. ham
5. jet
6. vet
7. bib
8. dad

Page 25

Short Vowels
Name
A Happy Thought:
sigh
I wouldn't know.
Laughing can be lots of fun.
1. pet
2. pig
3. jam
4. dog
5. cub
6. fish
7. lock
8. nut

Page 26

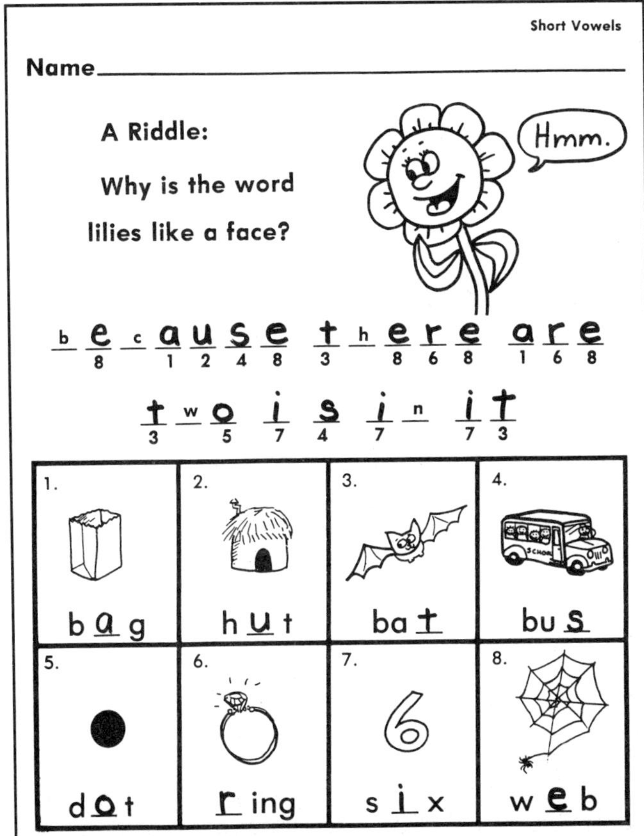

Short Vowels
Name
A Riddle:
Why is the word lilies like a face?
Hmm.
because there are two is in it
1. bag
2. hut
3. bat
4. bus
5. dot
6. ring
7. six
8. web

Page 27

Short Vowels
Name
A Tongue Twister:
For me?
a big baby buggy with rubber buggy bumpers
1. tub
2. hand
3. ring
4. net
5. pig
6. hat
7. dog
8. bell

Page 28

Answer Key

Short Vowels
Name
A Riddle:
What was the elephant doing on Route 495?
There he is!
about three miles
an hour
hug
bell
pin
ten
drum
top
king
map
NORTH
SOUTH

Page 29

Name
A Riddle:
What happens when an owl has a sore throat?
He doesn't give
a hoot.
king
well
cat
rug
sad
flag
hop
doll

Page 30

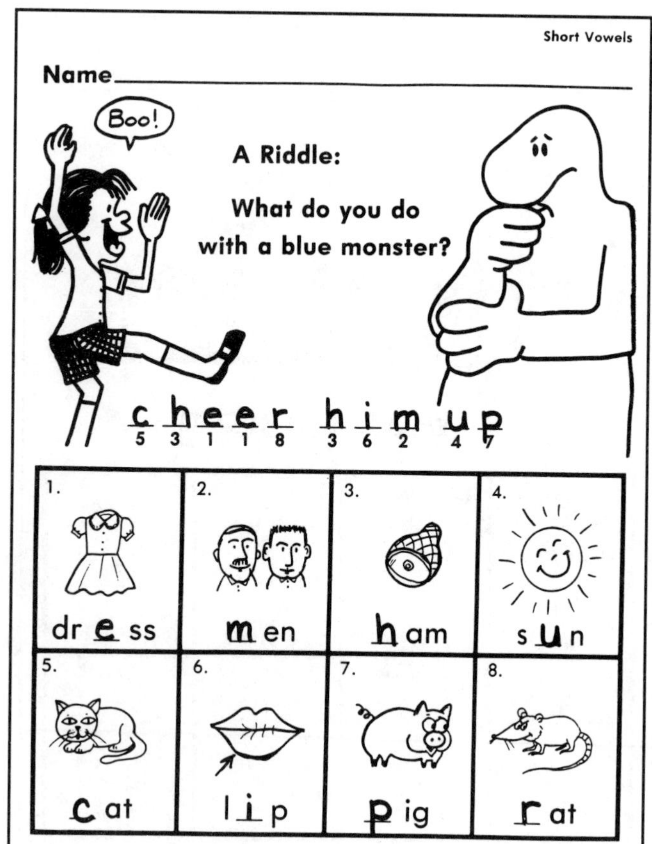

Short Vowels
Name
Boo!
A Riddle:
What do you do with a blue monster?
cheer him up
dress
men
ham
sun
cat
lip
pig
rat

Page 31

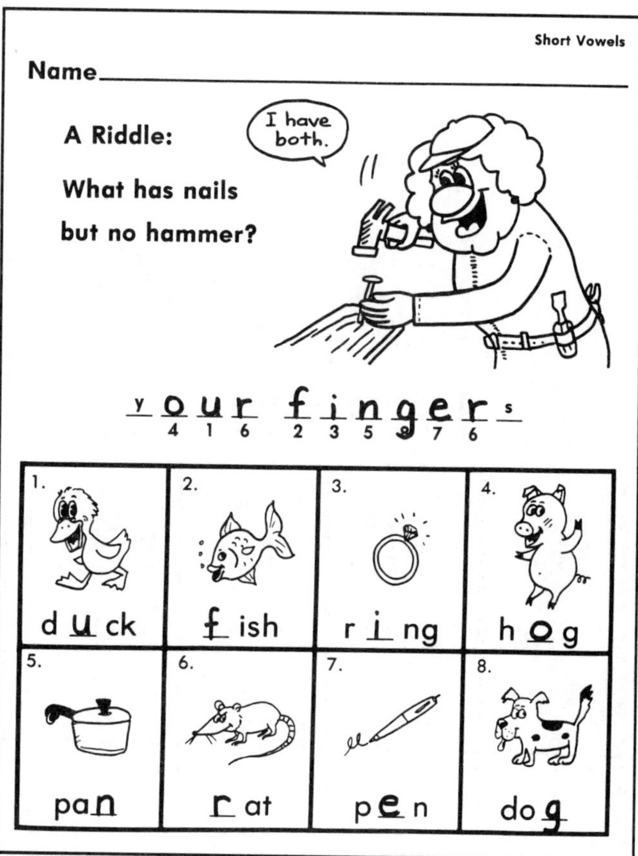

Short Vowels
Name
A Riddle:
What has nails but no hammer?
I have both.
your fingers
duck
fish
ring
hog
pan
rat
pen
dog

Page 32

Answer Key

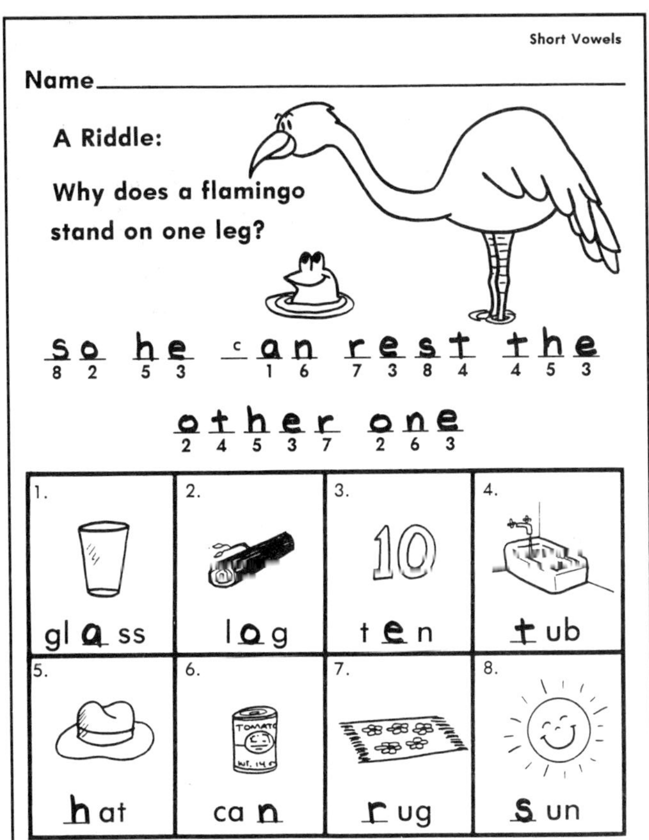
Short Vowels

Name

A Riddle:

Why does a flamingo stand on one leg?

so he can rest the other one

1. glass	2. log	3. ten	4. tub
5. hat	6. can	7. rug	8. sun

Page 33

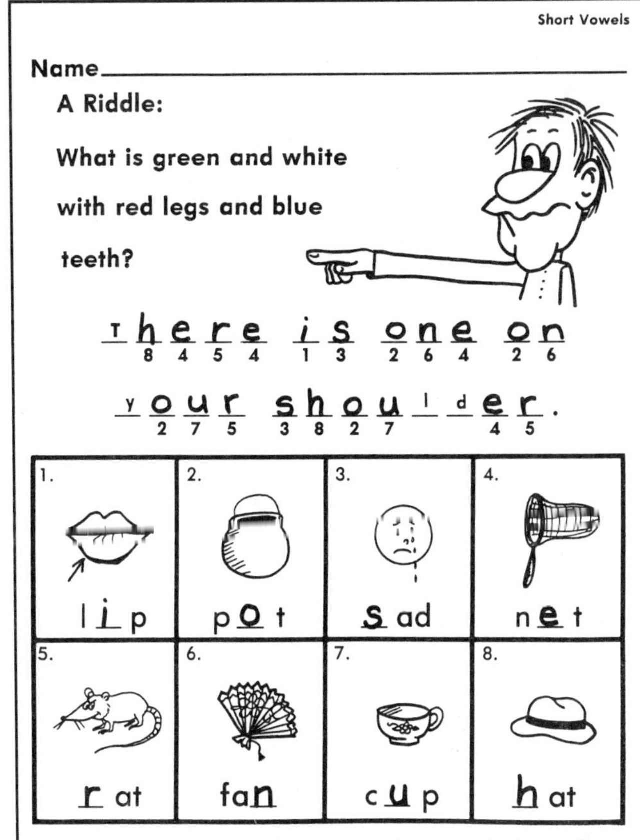
Short Vowels

Name

A Riddle:

What is green and white with red legs and blue teeth?

There is one on your shoulder.

1. lip	2. pot	3. sad	4. net
5. rat	6. fan	7. cup	8. hat

Page 34

Short Vowels

Name

A Happy Thought:

My teacher loves me.

1. mop	2. hat	3. cup	4. men
5. rat	6. bat	7. pen	8. log

Page 35

Short Vowels

Name

A Riddle:

What animal keeps time best?

I'm never late.

a watchdog

1. map	2. hat	3. dog	4. cup
5. bed	6. net	7. web	8. rug

Page 36

Answer Key

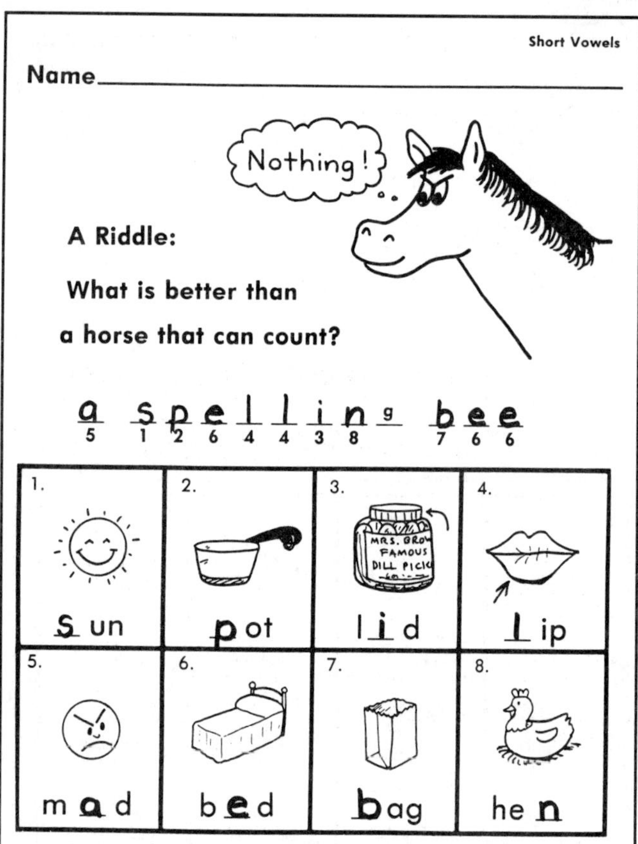
Short Vowels

Name

Nothing!

A Riddle:

What is better than a horse that can count?

a spelling bee

5 1 2 6 4 4 3 8 7 6 6

1. sun	2. pot	3. lid	4. lip
5. mad	6. bed	7. bag	8. hen

Page 37

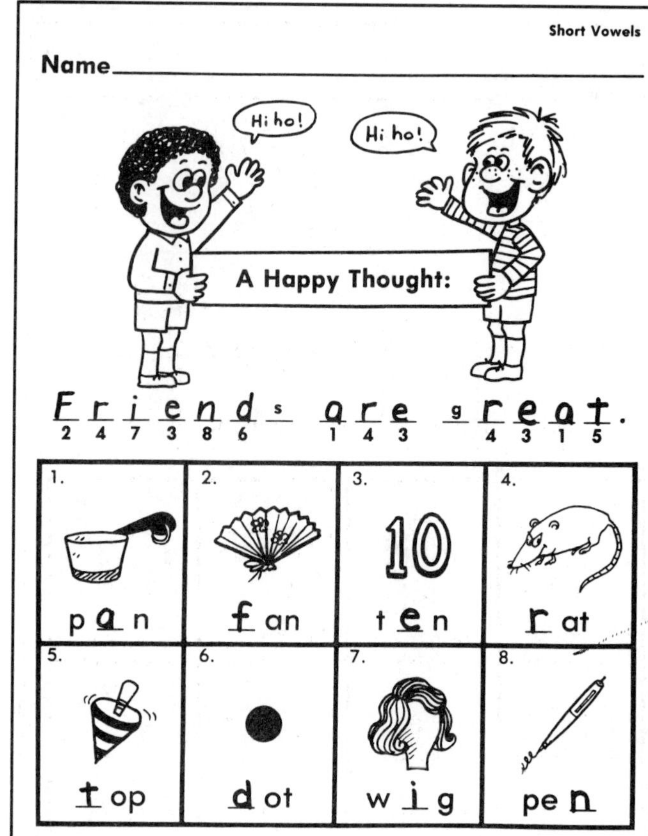
Short Vowels

Name

Hi ho!
Hi ho!

A Happy Thought:

Friends are great.

2 4 7 3 8 6 1 4 3 4 3 1 5

1. pan	2. fan	3. ten	4. rat
5. top	6. dot	7. wig	8. pen

Page 38

Short Vowels

Name

...And don't forget!

A Happy Thought:

Be kind to animals.

4 6 1 3 2 8 3 1 5 8 7

1. pin	2. top	3. nut	4. bag
5. mad	6. pen	7. six	8. cat

Page 39

Short Vowels

Name

scratch
scratch
itch
itch

A Riddle:

What did the dog say to the flea?

Don't bug me!

8 3 1 5 2 7 6 4

1. can	2. drum	3. frog	4. dress
5. bug	6. mop	7. pig	8. dad

Page 40

Answer Key

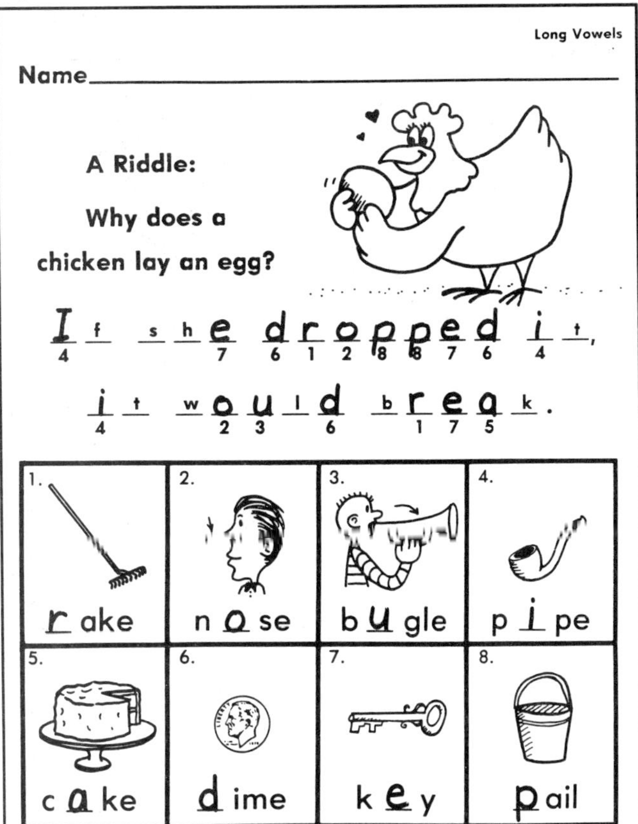

Long Vowels

Name

A Riddle:

Why does a chicken lay an egg?

If she dropped it, it would break.

1. rake 2. nose 3. bugle 4. pipe
5. cake 6. dime 7. key 8. pail

Page 41

Long Vowels

Name

Call the custodian!

A Tongue Twister:

The big bee buzzed by the blackboard.

1. phone 2. kite 3. ruler 4. bee
5. zebra 6. cake 7. dime 8. bike

Page 42

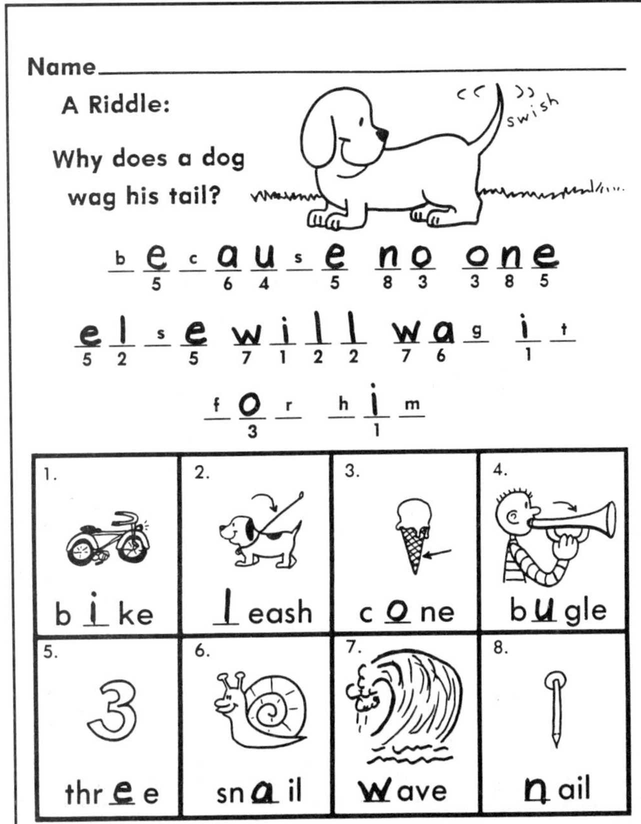

Name

A Riddle:

Why does a dog wag his tail?

swish

because no one else will wag it for him

1. bike 2. leash 3. cone 4. bugle
5. three 6. snail 7. wave 8. nail

Page 43

Name

A Riddle: What did the leopard say when it started to rain?

Ahhhh.

That hits the spots.

1. goat 2. seal 3. plate 4. ear
5. peach 6. nine 7. hose 8. toe

Page 44

Answer Key

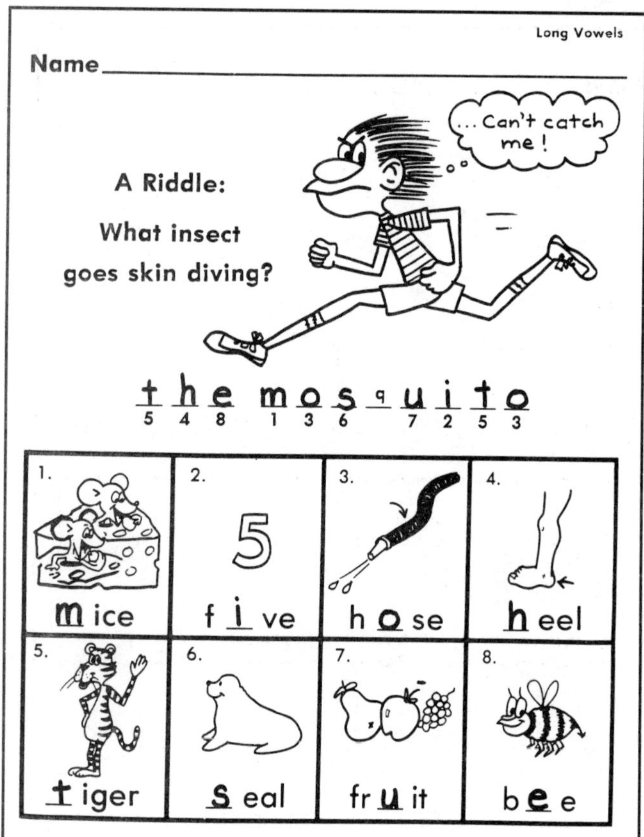

Long Vowels
Name
... Can't catch me!
A Riddle:
What insect goes skin diving?
the mosquito
5 4 8 1 3 6 7 2 5 3
1. mice
2. five
3. hose
4. heel
5. tiger
6. seal
7. fruit
8. bee

Page 45

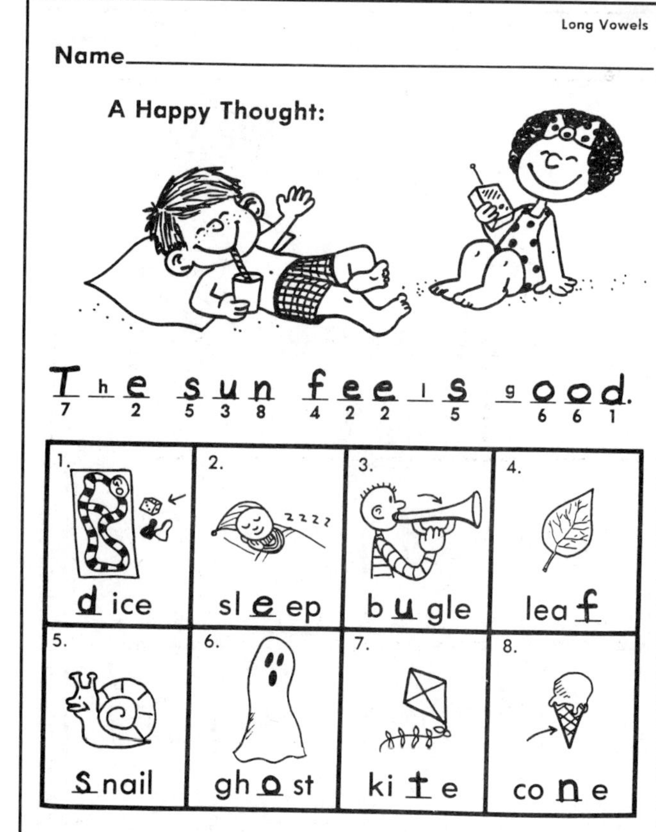

Long Vowels
Name
A Happy Thought:
The sun feels good.
7 2 5 3 8 4 2 2 5 6 6 1
1. dice
2. sleep
3. bugle
4. leaf
5. snail
6. ghost
7. kite
8. cone

Page 46

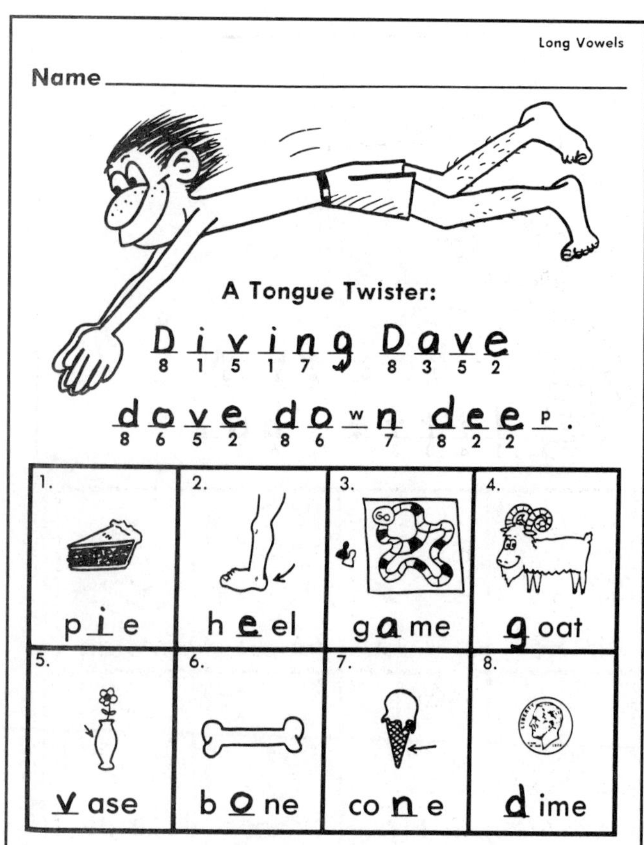

Long Vowels
Name
A Tongue Twister:
Diving Dave
8 1 5 1 7 4 8 3 5 2
dove down deep.
8 6 5 2 8 6 7 8 2 2
1. pie
2. heel
3. game
4. goat
5. vase
6. bone
7. cone
8. dime

Page 47

Name
..Now don't be afraid.
A Riddle:
What is the best way to talk to a monster?
long distance
4 1 6 8 2 3 6 5 7
1. goat
2. bike
3. baby
4. leaf
5. cone
6. nail
7. bee
8. dime

Page 48

Answer Key

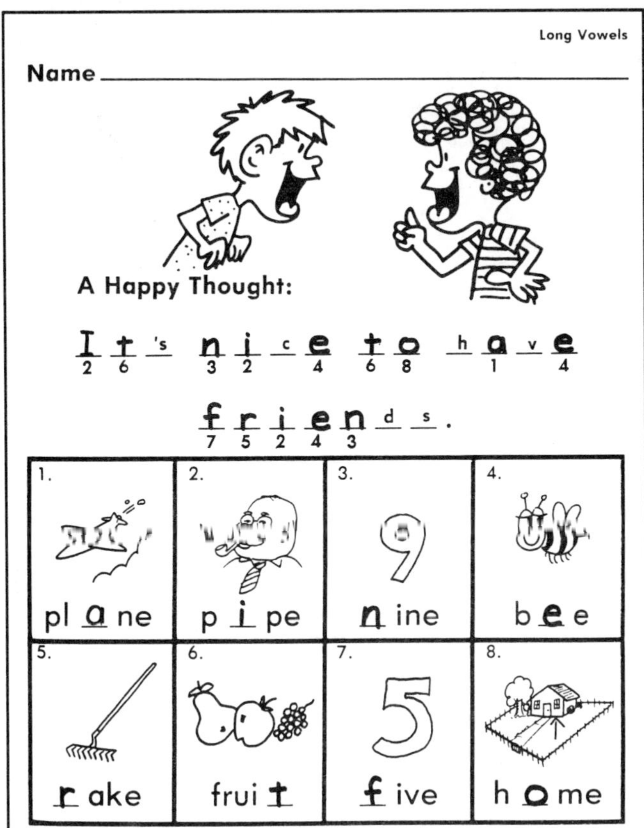
Long Vowels

Name ____________________

A Happy Thought:

It's nice to have friends.

1.	2.	3.	4.
pl a ne	p i pe	n ine	b e e
5.	6.	7.	8.
r ake	frui t	f ive	h o me

Page 49

Name ____________________

Eeeeeeek!

A Riddle:

What do you call a scared fish?

chicken of the sea

1.	2.	3.	4.
e ar	t i e	b o ne	f ive
5.	6.	7.	8.
n ail	sn a il	c ake	h ome

Page 50

Long Vowels

Name ____________________

Daffynition:

Kitchen

sprinkle
sprinkle

a shake and bake place

1.	2.	3.	4.
s nail	h ome	d ime	pla n e
5.	6.	7.	8.
k ite	p ie	t e eth	t a pe

Page 51

Long Vowels

Name ____________________

A Happy Thought:

Help keep the world beautiful! Do your part. Hurray!

Don't be a litter bug.

1.	2.	3.	4.
whee l	sh e ep	t ree	sm i le
5.	6.	7.	8.
tr a in	b low	t o e	b u gle

Page 52

Answer Key

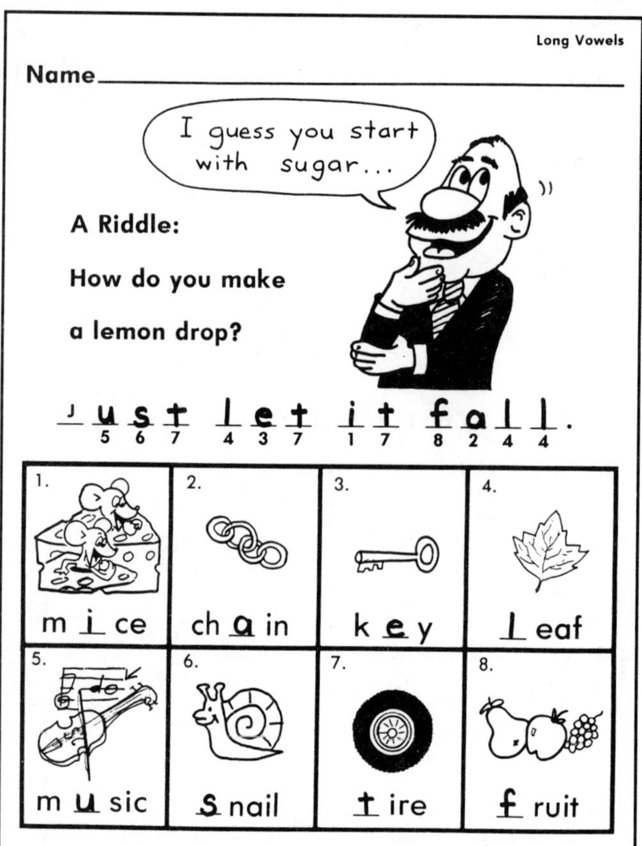

Long Vowels
Name
I guess you start with sugar...
A Riddle:
How do you make a lemon drop?
just let it fall.
5 6 7 4 3 7 1 7 8 2 4 4
1. mice
2. chain
3. key
4. leaf
5. music
6. snail
7. tire
8. fruit

Page 53

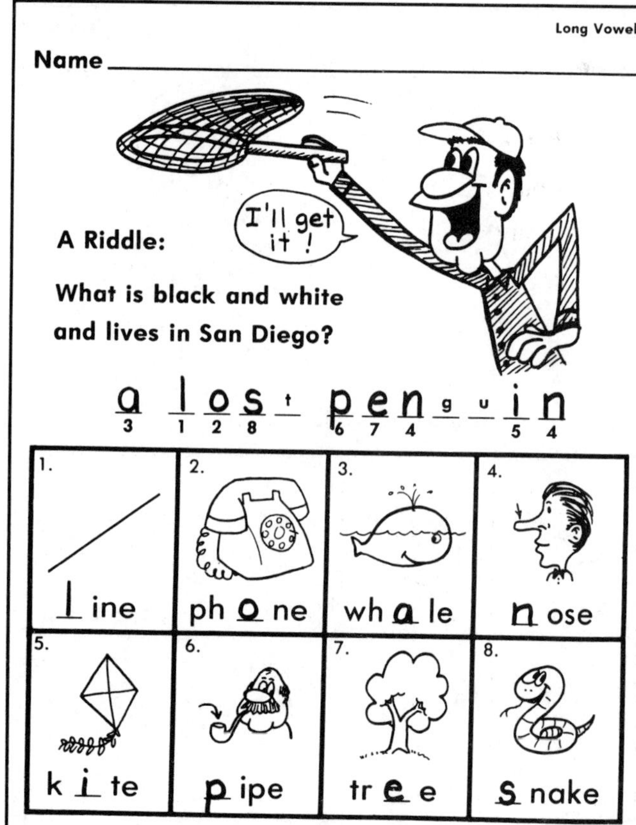

Long Vowels
Name
I'll get it!
A Riddle:
What is black and white and lives in San Diego?
a lost penguin
3 1 2 8 6 7 4 5 4
1. line
2. phone
3. whale
4. nose
5. kite
6. pipe
7. tree
8. snake

Page 54

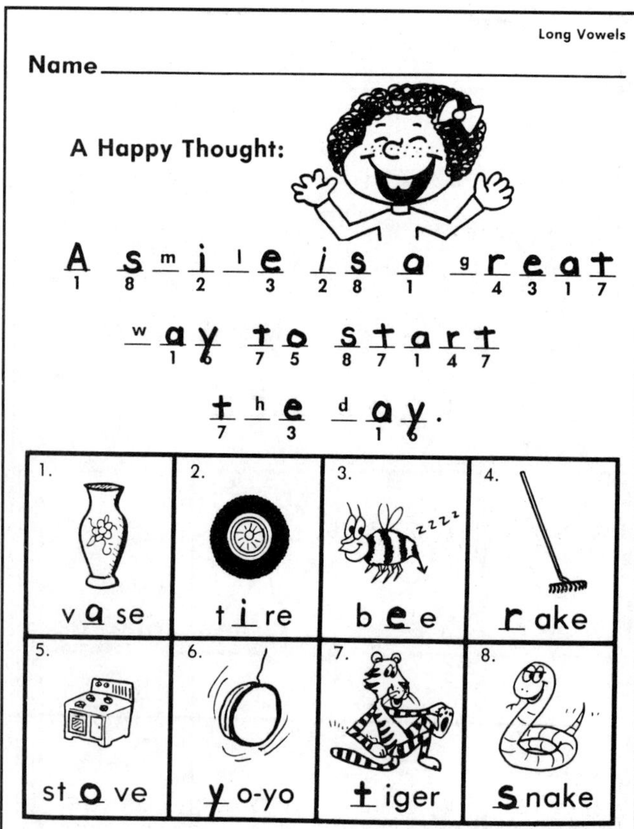

Long Vowels
Name
A Happy Thought:
A smile is a great
1 8 2 3 2 8 1 4 3 1 7
way to start
1 6 7 5 8 7 1 4 7
the day.
7 3 1 6
1. vase
2. tire
3. bee
4. rake
5. stove
6. yo-yo
7. tiger
8. snake

Page 55

Long Vowels
Name
WHAMO
SNAZ
A Tongue Twister:
Which wash
8 2 7 5 2 8 6 3 2
will wash well?
8 7 4 4 8 6 3 2 8 1 4 4
1. tree
2. hose
3. sleep
4. light
5. cake
6. tray
7. smile
8. wave

Page 56

Answer Key

Long Vowels

Name ______________________

A Riddle:

What is worse than finding a worm in an apple?

half a worm

1. hose	2. mail	3. home	4. table
5. leaf	6. ruler	7. weep	8. five

Page 57

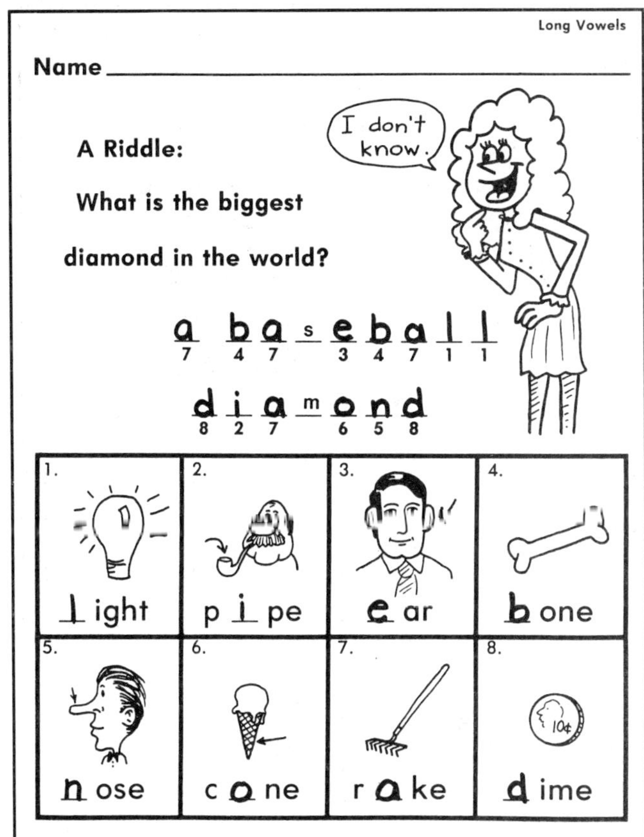

Long Vowels

Name ______________________

I don't know.

A Riddle:

What is the biggest diamond in the world?

a baseball diamond

1. light	2. pipe	3. ear	4. bone
5. nose	6. cone	7. rake	8. dime

Page 58

Long Vowels

Name ______________________

A Happy Thought:

Hello is a kind word.

1. note	2. three	3. tie	4. dime
5. rake	6. cage	7. line	8. leaf

Page 59

Long Vowels

Name ______________________

She sounds cute.

A Riddle:

What is brown and blue and has green teeth and a red nose.

There is one on your arm.

1. bugle	2. jeep	3. nail	4. plane
5. rake	6. bike	7. boat	8. tree

Page 60

Answer Key

Name ______________________ Skill: Phonics, Visual discrimination

Read the words in the Word Box.
Write the word that completes each sentence.
Circle the words in the puzzle.

1. I __want__ to play ball soon.
2. __When__ are they coming?
3. __Who__ is that man over there?
4. He __went__ home.
5. __What__ is his name?
6. __Where__ did he go after school?
7. I wonder __why__ I'm hungry?
8. __Which__ dog is yours?

Word Box
went
want
where
when
what
who
why
which

l	w	h	e	r	e	w
w	a	s	w	h	o	h
h	n	w	e	n	t	i
a	t	h	w	h	y	c
t	t	w	h	e	n	h

Page 61

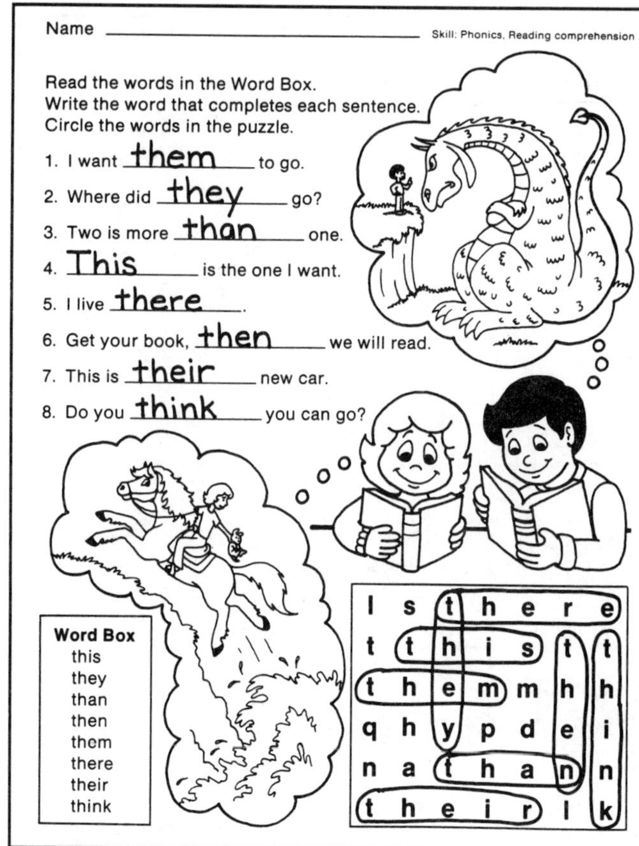

Name ______________________ Skill: Phonics, Reading comprehension

Read the words in the Word Box.
Write the word that completes each sentence.
Circle the words in the puzzle.

1. I want __them__ to go.
2. Where did __they__ go?
3. Two is more __than__ one.
4. __This__ is the one I want.
5. I live __there__.
6. Get your book, __then__ we will read.
7. This is __their__ new car.
8. Do you __think__ you can go?

Word Box
this
they
than
then
them
there
their
think

l	s	t	h	e	r	e
t	t	h	i	s	t	t
t	h	e	m	m	h	h
q	h	y	p	d	e	i
n	a	t	h	a	n	n
t	h	e	i	r	l	k

Page 62

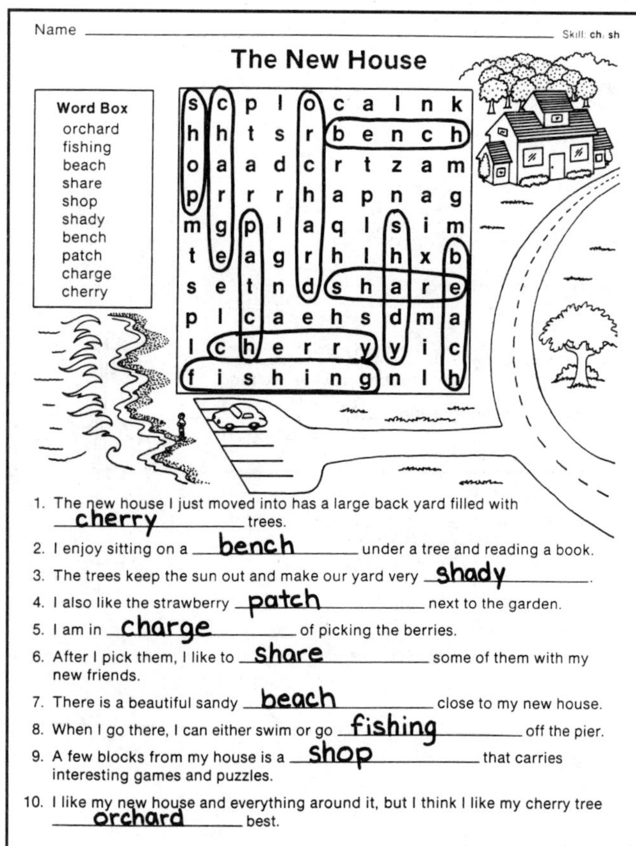

Name ______________________ Skill: ch, sh

The New House

Word Box
orchard
fishing
beach
share
shop
shady
bench
patch
charge
cherry

s	c	p	l	o	c	a	l	n	k
h	h	t	s	r	b	e	n	c	h
o	a	a	d	c	r	t	z	a	m
p	r	r	r	h	a	p	n	a	g
m	g	p	l	a	q	l	s	i	m
t	e	a	g	r	h	l	h	x	b
s	e	t	n	d	s	h	a	r	e
p	l	c	a	e	h	s	d	m	a
l	c	h	e	r	r	y	y	i	c
f	i	s	h	i	n	g	n	l	h

1. The new house I just moved into has a large back yard filled with __cherry__ trees.
2. I enjoy sitting on a __bench__ under a tree and reading a book.
3. The trees keep the sun out and make our yard very __shady__.
4. I also like the strawberry __patch__ next to the garden.
5. I am in __charge__ of picking the berries.
6. After I pick them, I like to __share__ some of them with my new friends.
7. There is a beautiful sandy __beach__ close to my new house.
8. When I go there, I can either swim or go __fishing__ off the pier.
9. A few blocks from my house is a __shop__ that carries interesting games and puzzles.
10. I like my new house and everything around it, but I think I like my cherry tree __orchard__ best.

Page 63

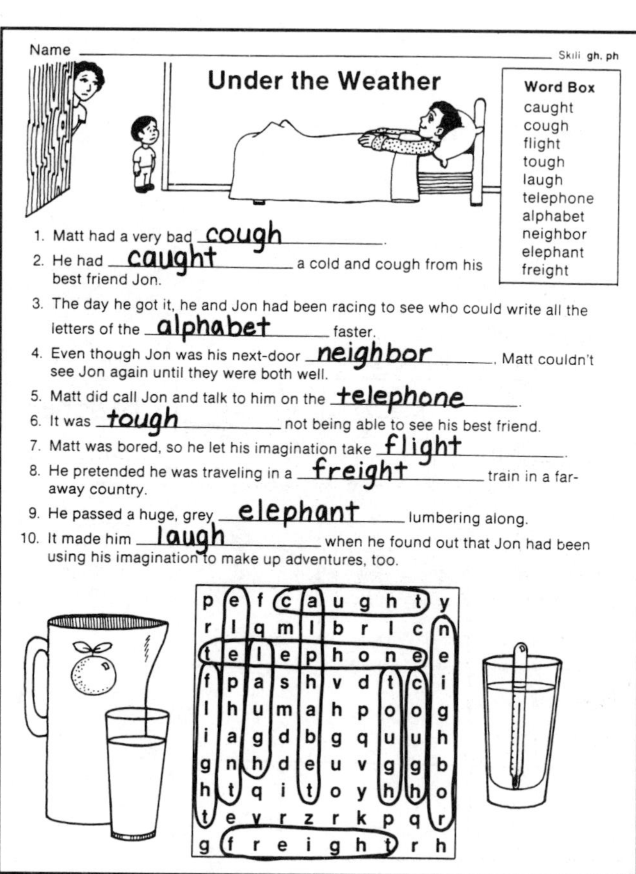

Name ______________________ Skill: gh, ph

Under the Weather

Word Box
caught
cough
flight
tough
laugh
telephone
alphabet
neighbor
elephant
freight

1. Matt had a very bad __cough__.
2. He had __caught__ a cold and cough from his best friend Jon.
3. The day he got it, he and Jon had been racing to see who could write all the letters of the __alphabet__ faster.
4. Even though Jon was his next-door __neighbor__, Matt couldn't see Jon again until they were both well.
5. Matt did call Jon and talk to him on the __telephone__.
6. It was __tough__ not being able to see his best friend.
7. Matt was bored, so he let his imagination take __flight__.
8. He pretended he was traveling in a __freight__ train in a far-away country.
9. He passed a huge, grey __elephant__ lumbering along.
10. It made him __laugh__ when he found out that Jon had been using his imagination to make up adventures, too.

p	e	f	c	a	u	g	h	t	y
r	l	q	m	l	b	r	l	c	n
t	e	l	e	p	h	o	n	e	e
f	p	a	s	h	v	d	t	c	i
l	h	u	m	a	h	p	o	o	g
i	a	g	d	b	g	q	u	u	h
g	n	h	d	e	u	v	g	g	b
h	t	q	i	t	o	y	h	h	o
t	e	y	r	z	r	k	p	q	r
g	f	r	e	i	g	h	t	r	h

Page 64

Answer Key

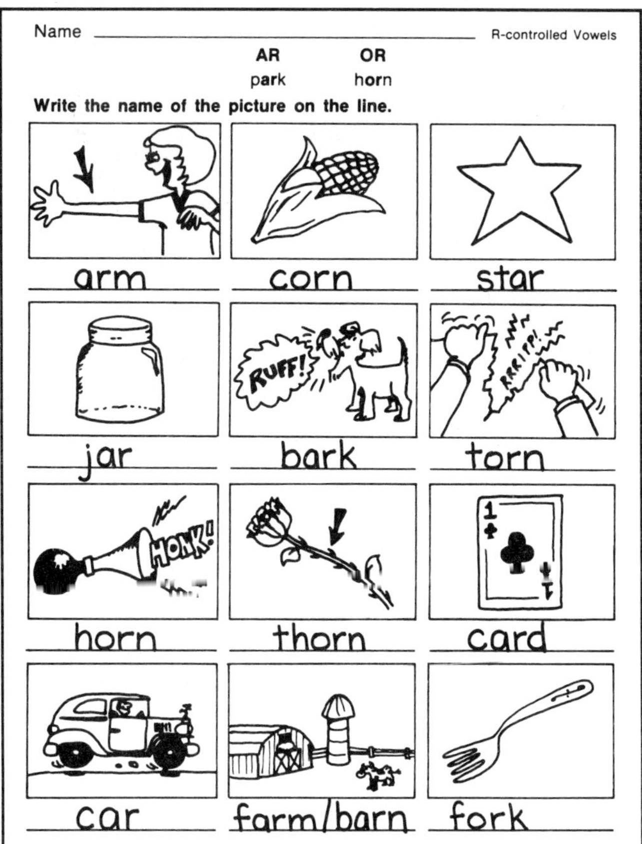

Name ______________________ R-controlled Vowels

AR park — OR horn

Write the name of the picture on the line.

RUFF!
RRRIP!
HONK!

arm	corn	star
jar	bark	torn
horn	thorn	card
car	farm/barn	fork

Page 65

Name ______________________ R-controlled Vowels Review

OR horn — UR turn — AR park

Circle the word that has the same R-sound as the picture. The first one is done for you.

1. Cows sleep in a ___.	her	(hard)	stir
2. Go to the ___.	mark	first	(horse)
3. Use my ___.	smart	(port)	hurry
4. I love ___.	(for)	start	dirt
5. Jam comes in a ___.	pork	(art)	her
6. Your dress is ___.	turn	park	(pork)
7. My sister is a ___.	(purple)	dark	fork
8. Our ___ can swim.	barn	port	(hurt)
9. Father is cooking a ___.	(fur)	horse	party
10. Mother is wearing a ___ coat.	farm	torn	(hurry)
11. Did you cut your ___?	turn	(park)	pork
12. Sue sent me a birthday ___.	(dark)	curl	stir

Page 66

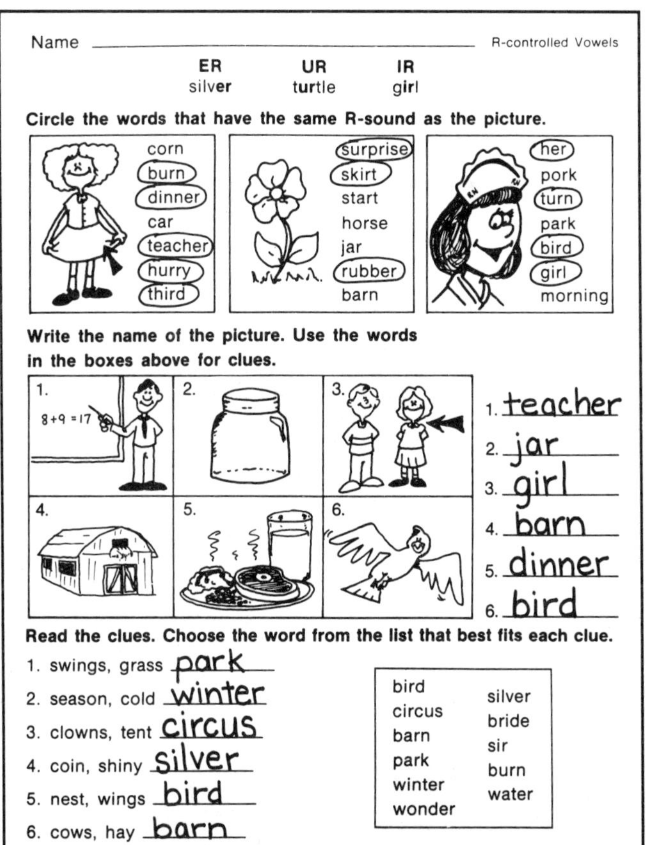

Name ______________________ R-controlled Vowels

ER silver — UR turtle — IR girl

Circle the words that have the same R-sound as the picture.

corn	(surprise)	(her)
(burn)	(skirt)	pork
(dinner)	start	(turn)
car	horse	park
(teacher)	jar	(bird)
(hurry)	(rubber)	(girl)
(third)	barn	morning

Write the name of the picture. Use the words in the boxes above for clues.

8+9 = 17

1. teacher
2. jar
3. girl
4. barn
5. dinner
6. bird

Read the clues. Choose the word from the list that best fits each clue.

1. swings, grass park
2. season, cold winter
3. clowns, tent circus
4. coin, shiny silver
5. nest, wings bird
6. cows, hay barn

bird	silver
circus	bride
barn	sir
park	burn
winter	water
wonder	

Page 67

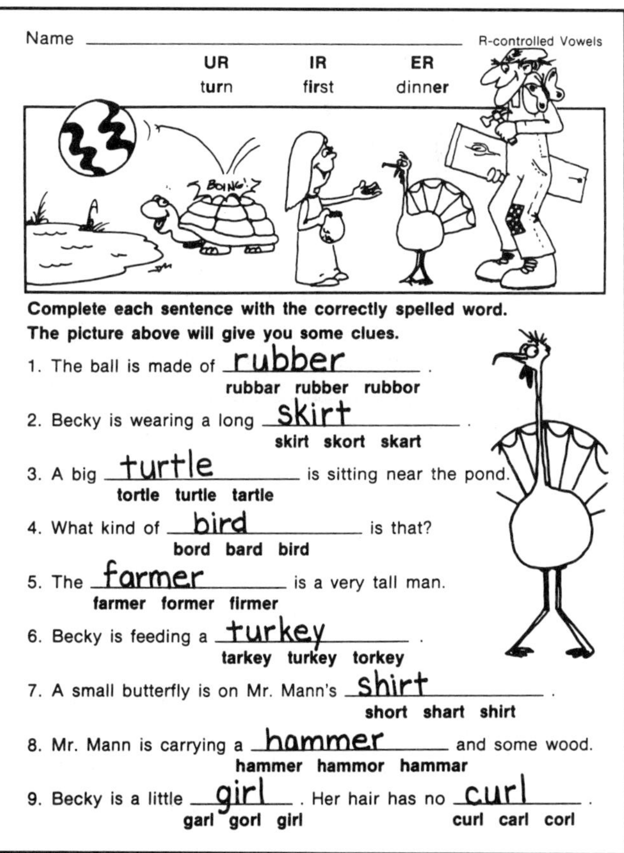

Name ______________________ R-controlled Vowels

UR turn — IR first — ER dinner

BOING!

Complete each sentence with the correctly spelled word. The picture above will give you some clues.

1. The ball is made of rubber.
   rubbar rubber rubbor
2. Becky is wearing a long skirt.
   skirt skort skart
3. A big turtle is sitting near the pond.
   tortle turtle tartle
4. What kind of bird is that?
   bord bard bird
5. The farmer is a very tall man.
   farmer former firmer
6. Becky is feeding a turkey.
   tarkey turkey torkey
7. A small butterfly is on Mr. Mann's shirt.
   short shart shirt
8. Mr. Mann is carrying a hammer and some wood.
   hammer hammor hammar
9. Becky is a little girl. Her hair has no curl.
   garl gorl girl — curl carl corl

Page 68

Answer Key

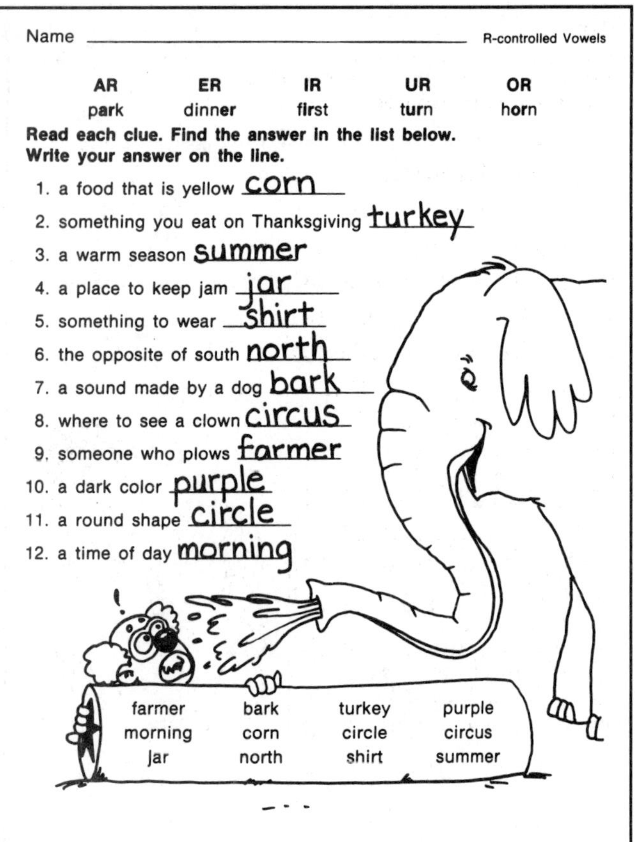

Name ______________ R-controlled Vowels

AR	ER	IR	UR	OR
park	dinner	first	turn	horn

Read each clue. Find the answer in the list below. Write your answer on the line.

1. a food that is yellow corn
2. something you eat on Thanksgiving turkey
3. a warm season summer
4. a place to keep jam jar
5. something to wear shirt
6. the opposite of south north
7. a sound made by a dog bark
8. where to see a clown circus
9. someone who plows farmer
10. a dark color purple
11. a round shape circle
12. a time of day morning

farmer	bark	turkey	purple
morning	corn	circle	circus
jar	north	shirt	summer

Page 69

Name ______________ Review

AR	IR	ER	UR	OR
park	first	dinner	turn	horn

Read each sentence. Choose the word that best completes the sentence and write it on the line.

1. Some cows live in a barn
   barn born burn
2. I'm going to be in the third grade.
   thorn turn third
3. If you don't hurry, we'll be late.
   hurry harry hurt
4. Corn is my favorite vegetable.
   core card corn
5. Did the house burn down?
   born bore burn
6. At night, it is very dark.
   dart dark dirt
7. Tim fell and hurt his knee.
   hard herb hurt
8. Take this pen and give it to her.
   her hare hire
9. A turtle crawls very slowly.
   turkey teacher turtle
10. Meat from pigs is called pork.
    port park pork
11. Let's have a surprise party for Anne.
    silver smart surprise
12. Don't swim out too far!
    fur first far

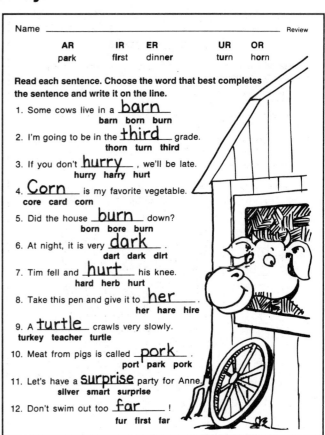

Page 70

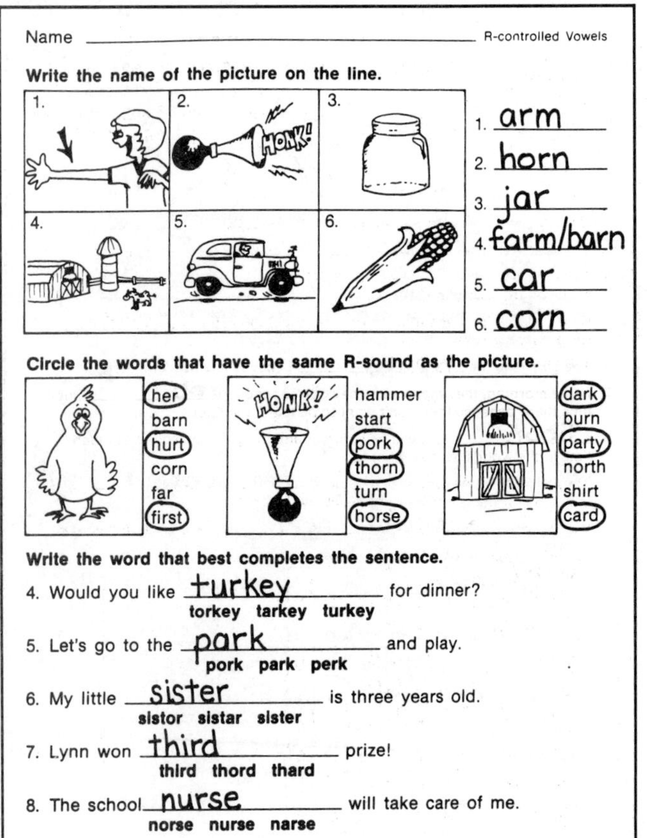

Name ______________ R-controlled Vowels

Write the name of the picture on the line.

1. arm
2. horn
3. jar
4. farm/barn
5. car
6. corn

HONK!

Circle the words that have the same R-sound as the picture.

(her)	hammer	(dark)
barn	start	burn
(hurt)	(pork)	(party)
corn	(thorn)	north
far	turn	shirt
(first)	(horse)	(card)

Write the word that best completes the sentence.

4. Would you like turkey for dinner?
   torkey tarkey turkey
5. Let's go to the park and play.
   pork park perk
6. My little sister is three years old.
   sistor sistar sister
7. Lynn won third prize!
   third thord thard
8. The school nurse will take care of me.
   norse nurse narse

Page 71

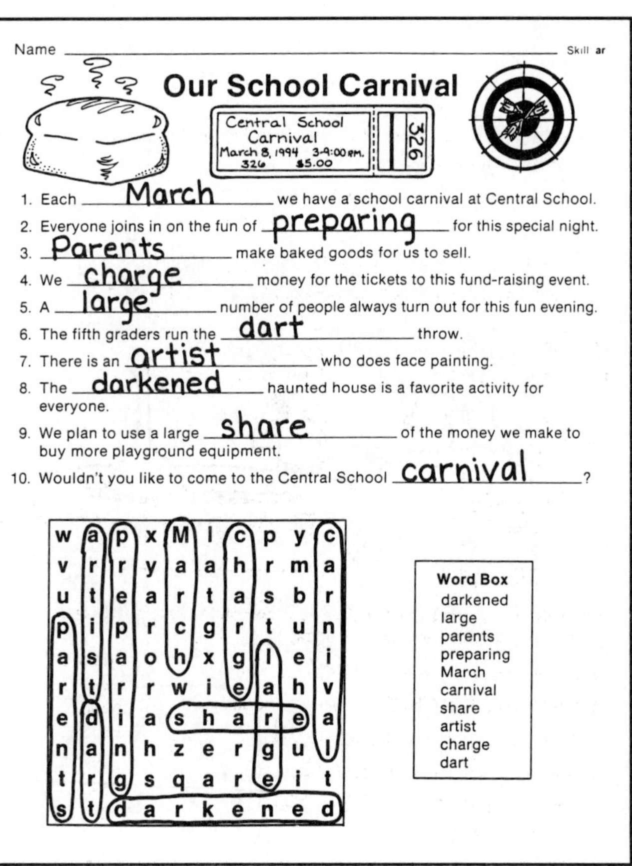

Name ______________ Skill ar

Our School Carnival

Central School Carnival
March 8, 1994 3-9:00 P.M.
326 $5.00
326

1. Each March we have a school carnival at Central School.
2. Everyone joins in on the fun of preparing for this special night.
3. Parents make baked goods for us to sell.
4. We charge money for the tickets to this fund-raising event.
5. A large number of people always turn out for this fun evening.
6. The fifth graders run the dart throw.
7. There is an artist who does face painting.
8. The darkened haunted house is a favorite activity for everyone.
9. We plan to use a large share of the money we make to buy more playground equipment.
10. Wouldn't you like to come to the Central School carnival?

w	a	p	x	M	l	c	p	y	c
v	r	r	y	a	a	h	r	m	a
u	t	e	a	r	t	a	s	b	r
p	i	p	r	c	g	r	t	u	n
a	s	a	o	h	x	g	l	e	i
r	t	r	r	w	i	e	a	h	v
e	d	i	a	s	h	a	r	e	a
n	a	n	h	z	e	r	g	u	l
t	r	g	s	q	a	r	e	i	t
s	t	d	a	r	k	e	n	e	d

Word Box
darkened
large
parents
preparing
March
carnival
share
artist
charge
dart

Page 72

Answer Key

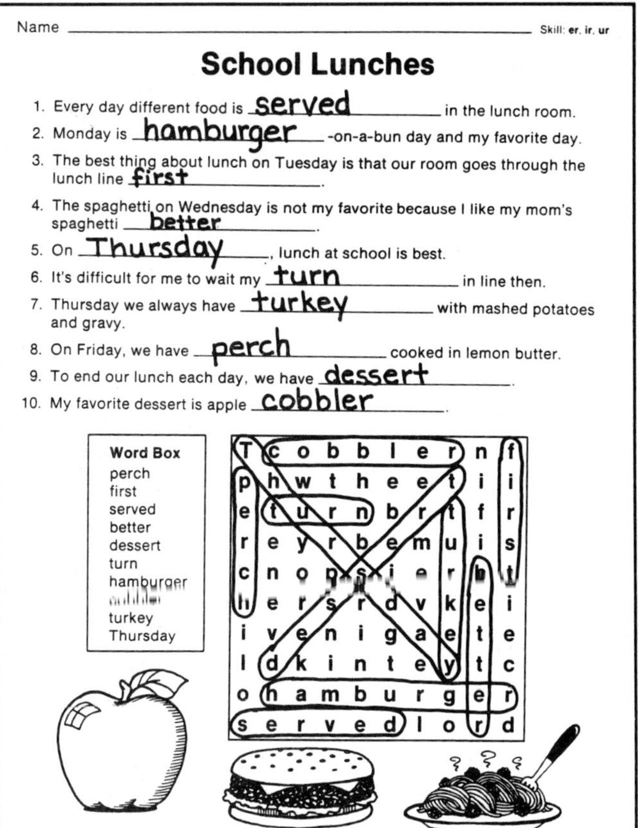

Name ______________________ Skill: er, ir, ur

School Lunches

1. Every day different food is served in the lunch room.
2. Monday is hamburger -on-a-bun day and my favorite day.
3. The best thing about lunch on Tuesday is that our room goes through the lunch line first.
4. The spaghetti on Wednesday is not my favorite because I like my mom's spaghetti better.
5. On Thursday, lunch at school is best.
6. It's difficult for me to wait my turn in line then.
7. Thursday we always have turkey with mashed potatoes and gravy.
8. On Friday, we have perch cooked in lemon butter.
9. To end our lunch each day, we have dessert.
10. My favorite dessert is apple cobbler.

Word Box
perch
first
served
better
dessert
turn
hamburger
cobbler
turkey
Thursday

T c o b b l e r n f
p h w t h e e t i i
e t u r n b r t f r
r e y r b e m u i s
c n o p s i e r h t
h e r s r d v k e i
i v e n i g a e t e
l d k i n t e y t c
o h a m b u r g e r
s e r v e d l o r d

Page 73

Name ______________________ Skill: Phonics, —oo vowel diagraph

Read the words in the Word Box.
Write the word that completes each sentence.
Circle the words in the puzzle.

1. I like to dive into the swimming pool.
2. My favorite food is pizza.
3. Do you like to look at the moon at night?
4. I bought a red balloon at the circus.
5. The funniest animals in the zoo are the monkeys.
6. Very soon it will be summer vacation.
7. What do you like best in school?
8. Mother said I could go, too.

Word Box

food	balloon	too	soon
zoo	pool	moon	school

b a l l o o n s
s p o o l o m o
c l n l s t u o
h z o o m o a n
o o f o o d c y
o o y h o o z g
l p e c n c h o
l o v s h t o o

Page 74

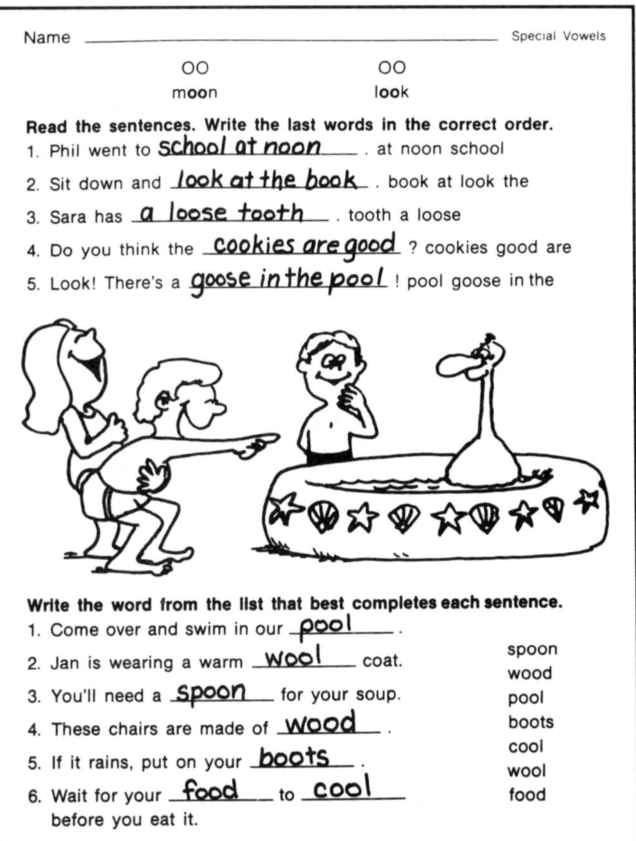

Name ______________________ Special Vowels

oo moon oo look

Read the sentences. Write the last words in the correct order.

1. Phil went to school at noon. at noon school
2. Sit down and look at the book. book at look the
3. Sara has a loose tooth. tooth a loose
4. Do you think the cookies are good? cookies good are
5. Look! There's a goose in the pool! pool goose in the

Write the word from the list that best completes each sentence.

1. Come over and swim in our pool.
2. Jan is wearing a warm wool coat.
3. You'll need a spoon for your soup.
4. These chairs are made of wood.
5. If it rains, put on your boots.
6. Wait for your food to cool before you eat it.

spoon
wood
pool
boots
cool
wool
food

Page 75

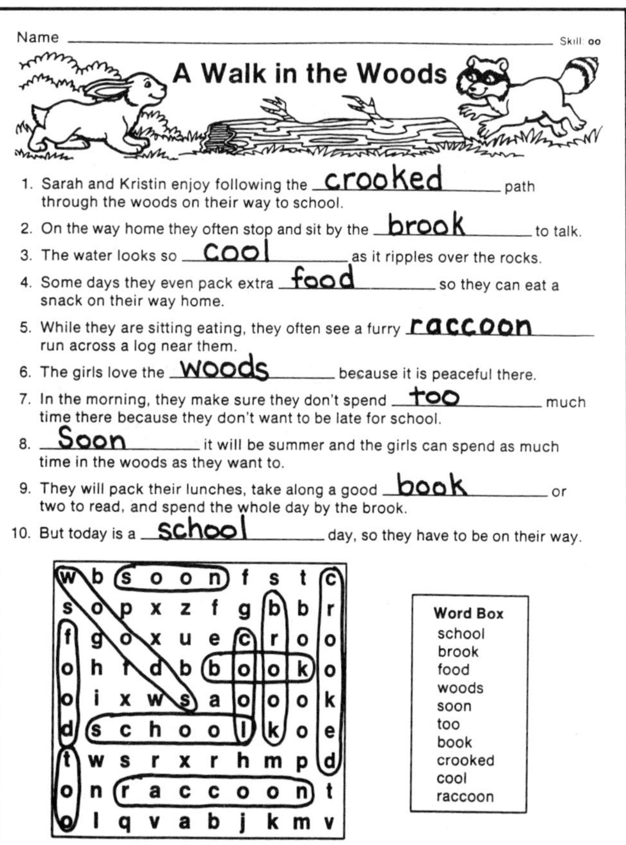

Name ______________________ Skill: oo

A Walk in the Woods

1. Sarah and Kristin enjoy following the crooked path through the woods on their way to school.
2. On the way home they often stop and sit by the brook to talk.
3. The water looks so cool as it ripples over the rocks.
4. Some days they even pack extra food so they can eat a snack on their way home.
5. While they are sitting eating, they often see a furry raccoon run across a log near them.
6. The girls love the woods because it is peaceful there.
7. In the morning, they make sure they don't spend too much time there because they don't want to be late for school.
8. Soon it will be summer and the girls can spend as much time in the woods as they want to.
9. They will pack their lunches, take along a good book or two to read, and spend the whole day by the brook.
10. But today is a school day, so they have to be on their way.

w b s o o n f s t c
s o p x z f g b b r
f g o x u e c r o o
o h f d b b o o k o
o i x w s a o o o k
d s c h o o l k o e
t w s r x r h m p d
o n r a c c o o n t
o l q v a b j k m v

Word Box
school
brook
food
woods
soon
too
book
crooked
cool
raccoon

Page 76

Answer Key

Name ______________ Special Vowels

The vowels **AU** and **AW** make a single sound. Say these words:
caught yawn

Read the sentences. Write the last words in the correct order.

1. Dan wakes up at dawn and yawns. yawns and dawn
2. My dog has claws on his paws. on paws claws his
3. Linda is the name of my daughter. my daughter of
4. No one knows how Paul caught a cold. caught Paul cold a
5. Can you draw a hawk? a hawk draw

My Pa has claws!

Write the word from the list that best completes each sentence.

6. The month after July is August.
7. Lynn can't go with us because she is sick.
8. On Sunday, Dad mows the lawn.
9. The season of fall is also called autumn.
10. Would you please draw me a picture?

paw
autumn
draw
August
because
lawn
auto

Page 77

Name ______________ Special Vowels

AW	AU	OO	OO
yawn	caught	book	moon

Find the word that matches each picture. Circle it.

1. clam, clock, (claw), clay
2. aunt, (auto), apart, ate
3. dinner, (daughter), dinosaur, driver
4. (tooth), tote, tool, toast
5. bowl, boom, boat, (boot)
6. yes, yarn, (yawn), yard
7. cork, cake, cool, (cook)
8. half, hoot, heap, (hoof)
9. spool, (spoon), spend, spine
10. fate, (foot), food, fool
11. (jaw), jam, jar, jay
12. dawn, dryer, drain, (draw)

What comes next? Choose your answers from the words you have circled above.

13. knife, fork, spoon
14. toe, heel, foot
15. cheek, chin, jaw
16. mother, sister, daughter

Page 78

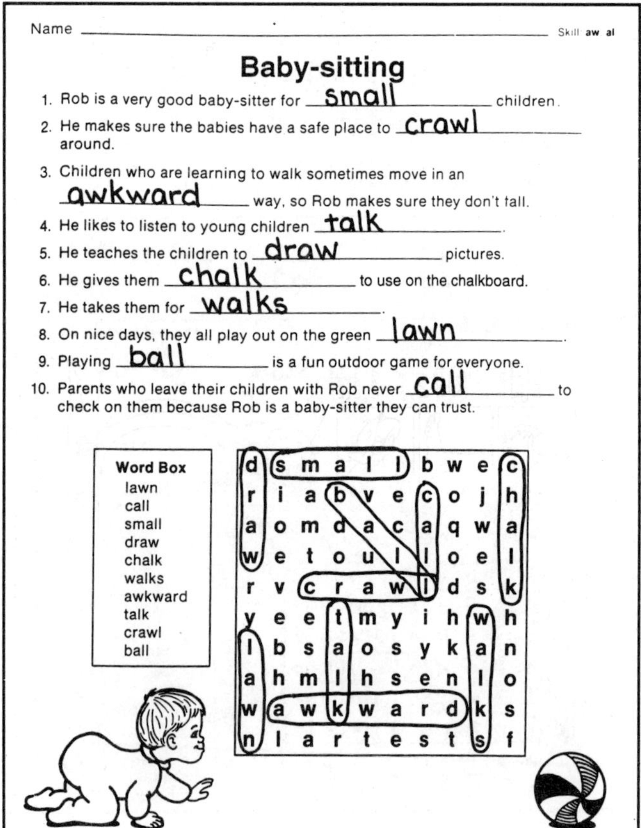

Name ______________ Skill aw al

Baby-sitting

1. Rob is a very good baby-sitter for small children.
2. He makes sure the babies have a safe place to crawl around.
3. Children who are learning to walk sometimes move in an awkward way, so Rob makes sure they don't fall.
4. He likes to listen to young children talk.
5. He teaches the children to draw pictures.
6. He gives them chalk to use on the chalkboard.
7. He takes them for walks.
8. On nice days, they all play out on the green lawn.
9. Playing ball is a fun outdoor game for everyone.
10. Parents who leave their children with Rob never call to check on them because Rob is a baby-sitter they can trust.

Word Box
lawn
call
small
draw
chalk
walks
awkward
talk
crawl
ball

d	s	m	a	l	l	b	w	e	c
r	i	a	b	v	e	c	o	j	h
a	o	m	d	a	c	a	q	w	a
w	e	t	o	u	l	l	o	e	l
r	v	c	r	a	w	l	d	s	k
y	e	e	t	m	y	i	h	w	h
l	b	s	a	o	s	y	k	a	n
a	h	m	l	h	s	e	n	l	o
w	a	w	k	w	a	r	d	k	s
n	l	a	r	t	e	s	t	s	f

Page 79

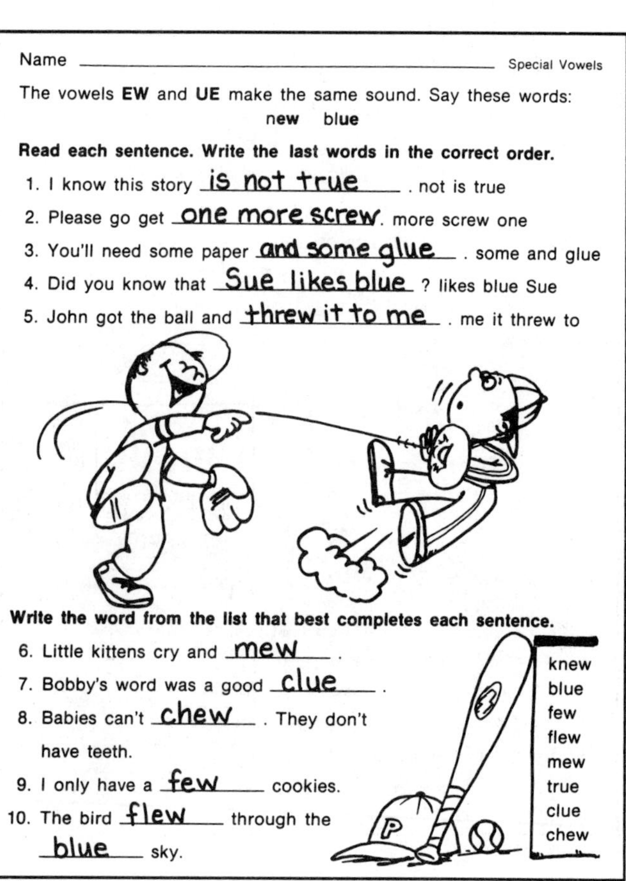

Name ______________ Special Vowels

The vowels **EW** and **UE** make the same sound. Say these words:
new blue

Read each sentence. Write the last words in the correct order.

1. I know this story is not true. not is true
2. Please go get one more screw. more screw one
3. You'll need some paper and some glue. some and glue
4. Did you know that Sue likes blue? likes blue Sue
5. John got the ball and threw it to me. me it threw to

Write the word from the list that best completes each sentence.

6. Little kittens cry and mew.
7. Bobby's word was a good clue.
8. Babies can't chew. They don't have teeth.
9. I only have a few cookies.
10. The bird flew through the blue sky.

knew
blue
few
flew
mew
true
clue
chew

P

Page 80

Answer Key

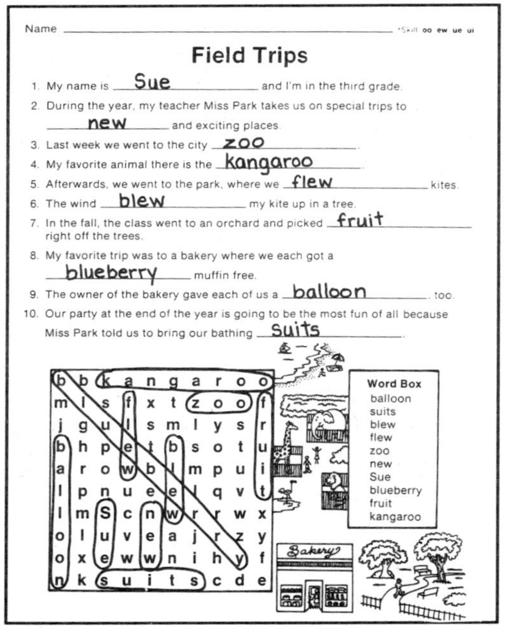

Name ______ Skill: oo ew ue ui

Field Trips

1. My name is <u>Sue</u> and I'm in the third grade.
2. During the year, my teacher Miss Park takes us on special trips to <u>new</u> and exciting places.
3. Last week we went to the city <u>zoo</u>.
4. My favorite animal there is the <u>kangaroo</u>.
5. Afterwards, we went to the park, where we <u>flew</u> kites.
6. The wind <u>blew</u> my kite up in a tree.
7. In the fall, the class went to an orchard and picked <u>fruit</u> right off the trees.
8. My favorite trip was to a bakery where we each got a <u>blueberry</u> muffin free.
9. The owner of the bakery gave each of us a <u>balloon</u>, too.
10. Our party at the end of the year is going to be the most fun of all because Miss Park told us to bring our bathing <u>suits</u>.

b b k a n g a r o o
m l s f x t z o o f
j g u l s m l y s r
b h p e t b s o t u
a r o w b l m p u i
l p n u e e l q v t
l m S c n w r r w x
o l u v e a j r z y
o x e w w n i h y f
n k s u i t s c d e

Word Box: balloon, suits, blew, flew, zoo, new, Sue, blueberry, fruit, kangaroo

Page 81

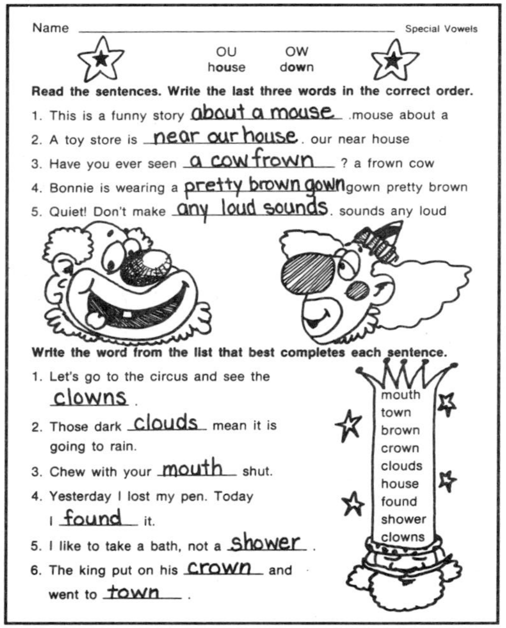

Name ______ Special Vowels

OU house — OW down

Read the sentences. Write the last three words in the correct order.

1. This is a funny story <u>about a mouse</u>. mouse about a
2. A toy store is <u>near our house</u>. our near house
3. Have you ever seen <u>a cow frown</u>? a frown cow
4. Bonnie is wearing a <u>pretty brown gown</u>. gown pretty brown
5. Quiet! Don't make <u>any loud sounds</u>. sounds any loud

Write the word from the list that best completes each sentence.

1. Let's go to the circus and see the <u>clowns</u>.
2. Those dark <u>clouds</u> mean it is going to rain.
3. Chew with your <u>mouth</u> shut.
4. Yesterday I lost my pen. Today I <u>found</u> it.
5. I like to take a bath, not a <u>shower</u>.
6. The king put on his <u>crown</u> and went to <u>town</u>.

mouth, town, brown, crown, clouds, house, found, shower, clowns

Page 82

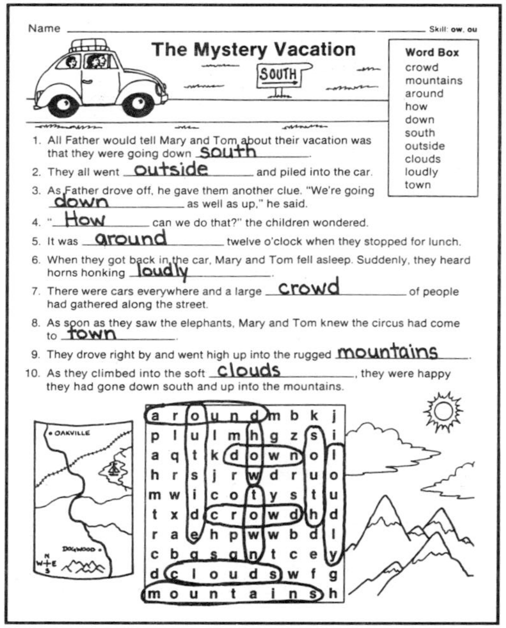

Name ______ Skill: ow, ou

The Mystery Vacation

SOUTH

Word Box: crowd, mountains, around, how, down, south, outside, clouds, loudly, town

1. All Father would tell Mary and Tom about their vacation was that they were going down <u>south</u>.
2. They all went <u>outside</u> and piled into the car.
3. As Father drove off, he gave them another clue. "We're going <u>down</u> as well as up," he said.
4. "<u>How</u> can we do that?" the children wondered.
5. It was <u>around</u> twelve o'clock when they stopped for lunch.
6. When they got back in the car, Mary and Tom fell asleep. Suddenly, they heard horns honking <u>loudly</u>.
7. There were cars everywhere and a large <u>crowd</u> of people had gathered along the street.
8. As soon as they saw the elephants, Mary and Tom knew the circus had come to <u>town</u>.
9. They drove right by and went high up into the rugged <u>mountains</u>.
10. As they climbed into the soft <u>clouds</u>, they were happy they had gone down south and up into the mountains.

OAKVILLE
DOGWOOD

a r o u n d m b k j
p l u l m h g z s l
a q t k d o w n o l
h r s j r w d r u o
m w i c o t y s t u
t x d c r o w d h d
r a e h p w w b d l
c b g s g n t c e y
d c l o u d s w f g
m o u n t a i n s h

Page 83

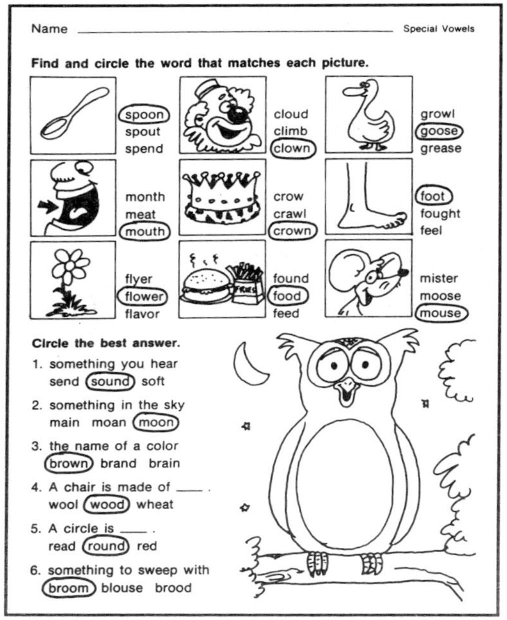

Name ______ Special Vowels

Find and circle the word that matches each picture.

(spoon) spout spend	cloud climb (clown)	growl (goose) grease
month meat (mouth)	crow crawl (crown)	(foot) fought feel
flyer (flower) flavor	found (food) feed	mister moose (mouse)

Circle the best answer.

1. something you hear — send (sound) soft
2. something in the sky — main moan (moon)
3. the name of a color — (brown) brand brain
4. A chair is made of ___. — wool (wood) wheat
5. A circle is ___. — read (round) red
6. something to sweep with — (broom) blouse brood

Page 84

Name ______ Special Vowels

Write the word that best fits in each sentence below. Cross out the word that does not belong. The picture will give you clues.

1. Jennifer is wearing a <u>crown</u>. ~~crane~~, crown
2. There is only one <u>cloud</u> in the sky. cloud, ~~clown~~
3. Mark <u>threw</u> a bone to the dog. threw, ~~three~~
4. Do you think the dog will <u>chew</u> on the bone? ~~chin~~, chew
5. The sun and the ball are <u>round</u>. ~~rolled~~, round
6. Jennifer's <u>blouse</u> has a red <u>flower</u> on it. ~~blush~~, blouse — flower, ~~floor~~
7. The <u>mouse</u> didn't scare our <u>cow</u> at all. mouse, ~~moose~~ — cow, ~~caw~~
8. The dog's name is <u>Sue</u>. ~~Saw~~, Sue

Page 85

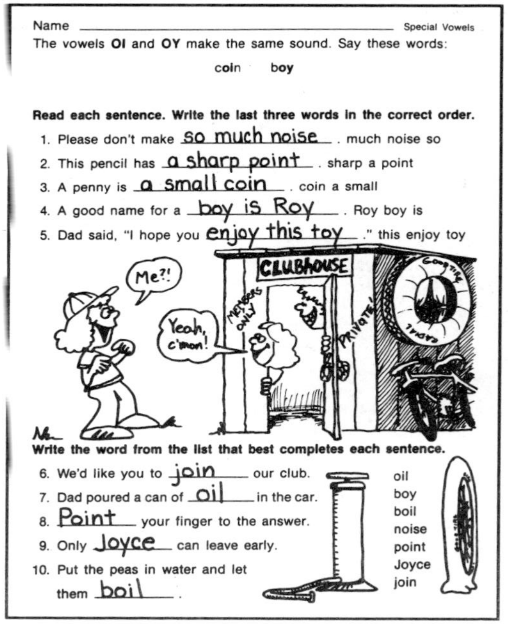

Name ______ Special Vowels

The vowels **OI** and **OY** make the same sound. Say these words:

coin boy

Read each sentence. Write the last three words in the correct order.

1. Please don't make <u>so much noise</u>. much noise so
2. This pencil has <u>a sharp point</u>. sharp a point
3. A penny is <u>a small coin</u>. coin a small
4. A good name for a <u>boy is Roy</u>. Roy boy is
5. Dad said, "I hope you <u>enjoy this toy</u>." this enjoy toy

Me?!
Yeah, c'mon!
CLUBHOUSE
MEMBERS ONLY
PRIVATE!

Write the word from the list that best completes each sentence.

6. We'd like you to <u>join</u> our club.
7. Dad poured a can of <u>oil</u> in the car.
8. <u>Point</u> your finger to the answer.
9. Only <u>Joyce</u> can leave early.
10. Put the peas in water and let them <u>boil</u>.

oil, boy, boil, noise, point, Joyce, join

Page 86

Answer Key

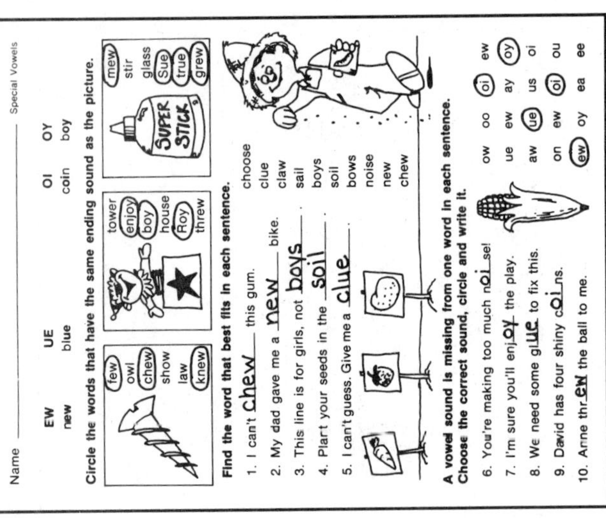

Page 89

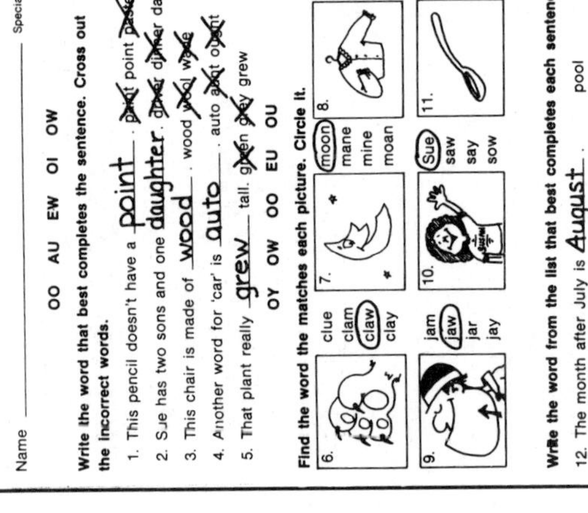

Page 92

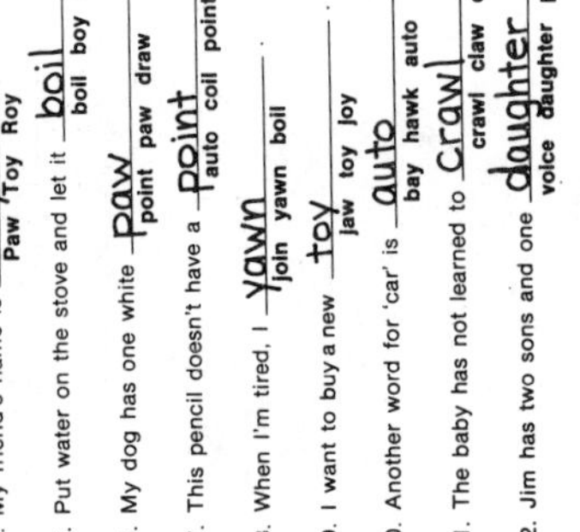

Page 88

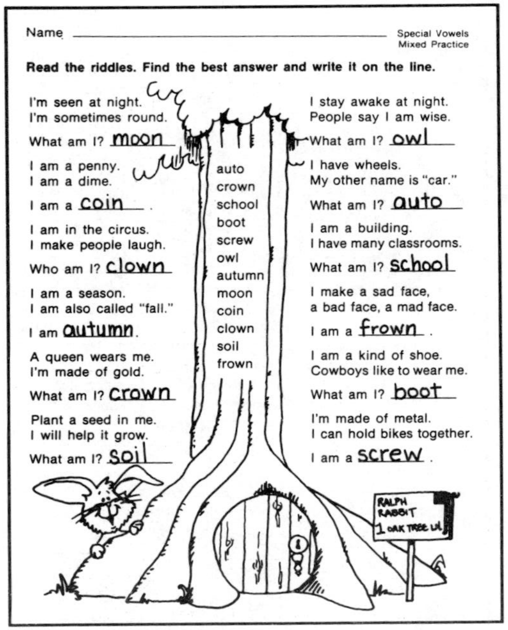

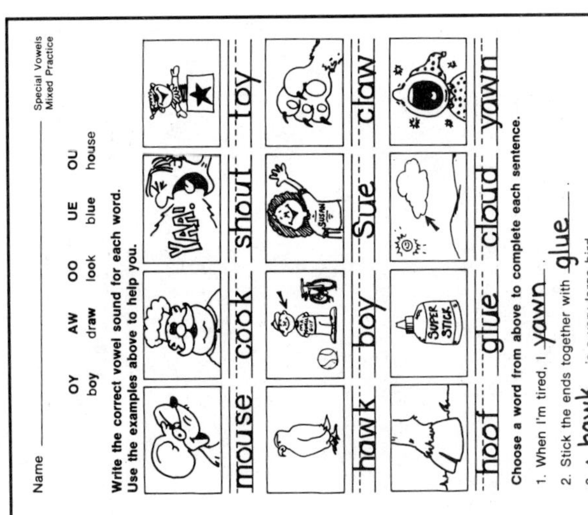

Page 91

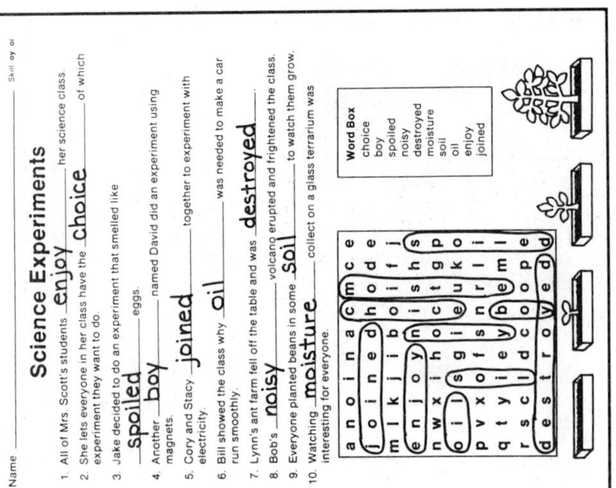

Page 87

Page 90

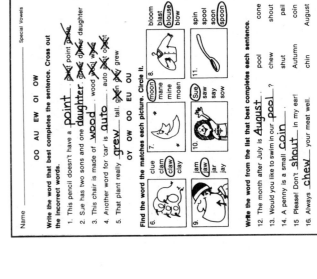

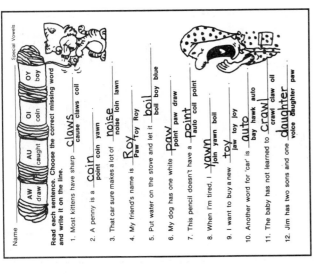

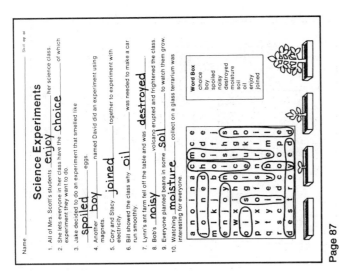

Answer Key

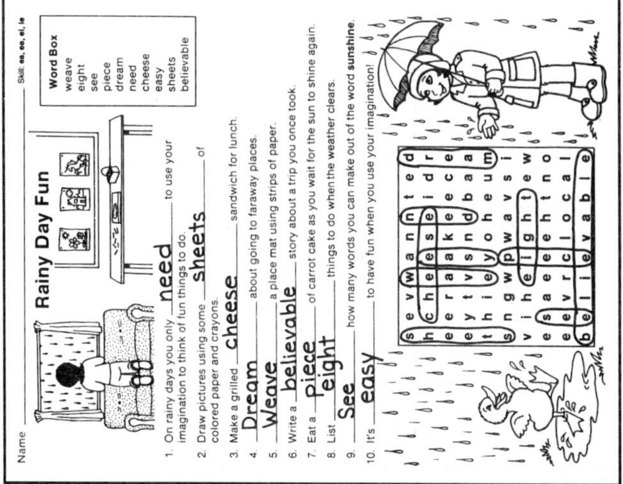

Name ______ Skill: ea, ee, ei, ie

Rainy Day Fun

Word Box: weave, eight, see, piece, dream, need, cheese, easy, sheets, believable

1. On rainy days you only need to use your imagination to think of fun things to do.
2. Draw pictures using some sheets of colored paper and crayons.
3. Make a grilled cheese sandwich for lunch.
4. Dream about going to faraway places.
5. Weave a place mat using strips of paper.
6. Write a believable story about a trip you once took.
7. Eat a piece of carrot cake as you wait for the sun to shine again.
8. List eight things to do when the weather clears.
9. See how many words you can make out of the word **sunshine**.
10. It's easy to have fun when you use your imagination!

Page 93

Name ______ Skill: ci, si, ti

The Surprise Party

Word Box: occasion, suspicious, musician, directions, patient, invitation, special, mission, permission, mention

Welcome Home Gail!

1. Sandy had to write one more invitation for Gail's surprise party.
2. She put a map with directions to Gail's house in the envelope and she was finished.
3. This was to be a very special party.
4. Gail had been a patient in the hospital for many weeks and now she was coming home.
5. Sandy had told everyone not to mention the party to Gail.
6. A musician had been hired to play.
7. Gail's mother had given Gail's friends permission to give her a kitten as a welcome-home gift.
8. Gail wasn't at all suspicious as she opened the door.
9. The mission to keep the party a surprise had succeeded.
10. This was a happy occasion for Gail and everyone.

Page 94

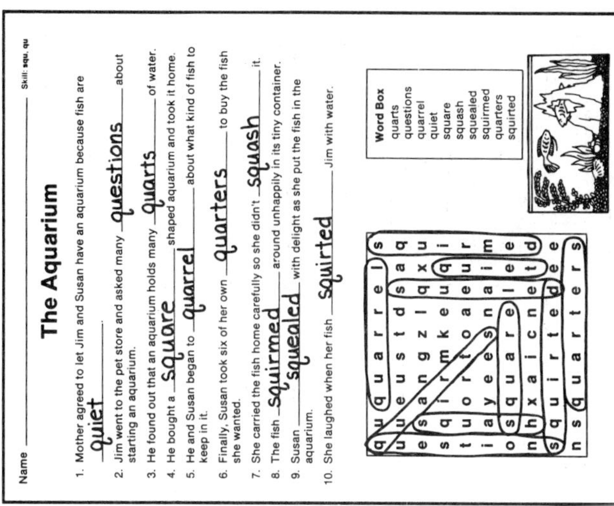

Name ______ Skill: squ, qu

The Aquarium

1. Mother agreed to let Jim and Susan have an aquarium because fish are quiet.
2. Jim went to the pet store and asked many questions about starting an aquarium.
3. He found out that an aquarium holds many quarts of water.
4. He bought a square shaped aquarium and took it home.
5. He and Susan began to quarrel about what kind of fish to keep in it.
6. Finally, Susan took six of her own quarters to buy the fish she wanted.
7. She carried the fish home carefully so she didn't squash it.
8. The fish squirmed around unhappily in its tiny container.
9. Susan squealed with delight as she put the fish in the aquarium.
10. She laughed when her fish squirted Jim with water.

Word Box: quarts, questions, quarrel, quiet, square, squash, squealed, squirmed, quarters, squirted

Page 95

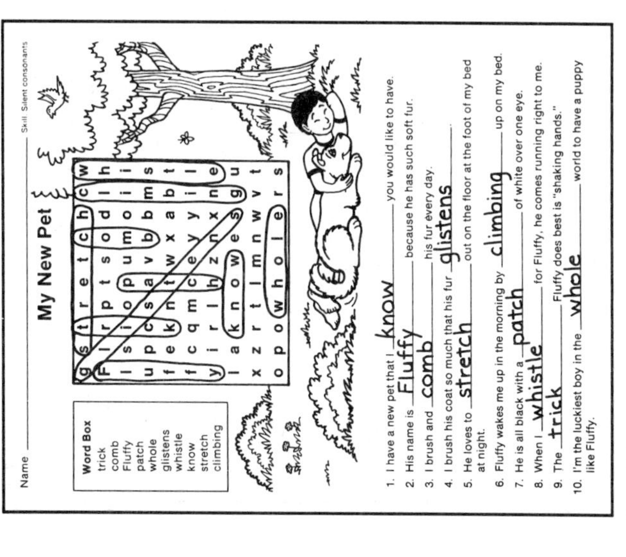

Name ______ Skill: Silent consonants

My New Pet

Word Box: trick, comb, Fluffy, patch, whole, glistens, whistle, know, stretch, climbing

1. I have a new pet that I know you would like to have.
2. His name is Fluffy because he has such soft fur.
3. I brush and comb his fur every day.
4. I brush his coat so much that his fur glistens.
5. He loves to stretch out on the floor at the foot of my bed at night.
6. Fluffy wakes me up in the morning by climbing up on my bed.
7. He is all black with a patch of white over one eye.
8. When I whistle for Fluffy, he comes running right to me.
9. The trick Fluffy does best is "shaking hands."
10. I'm the luckiest boy in the whole world to have a puppy like Fluffy.

Page 96

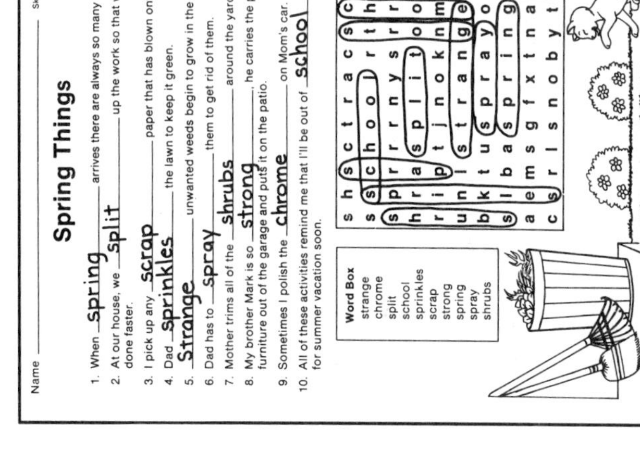

Name ______ Skill: 3-letter blends

Spring Things

1. When spring arrives there are always so many things to do.
2. At our house, we split up the work so that we can get it done faster.
3. I pick up any scrap paper that has blown onto the lawn.
4. Dad sprinkles the lawn to keep it green.
5. Strange unwanted weeds begin to grow in the grass.
6. Dad has to spray them to get rid of them.
7. Mother trims all of the shrubs around the yard.
8. My brother Mark is so strong, he carries the patio furniture out of the garage and puts it on the patio.
9. Sometimes I polish the chrome on Mom's car.
10. All of these activities remind me that I'll be out of school for summer vacation soon.

Word Box: strange, chrome, split, school, sprinkles, scrap, strong, spring, spray, shrubs

Page 97

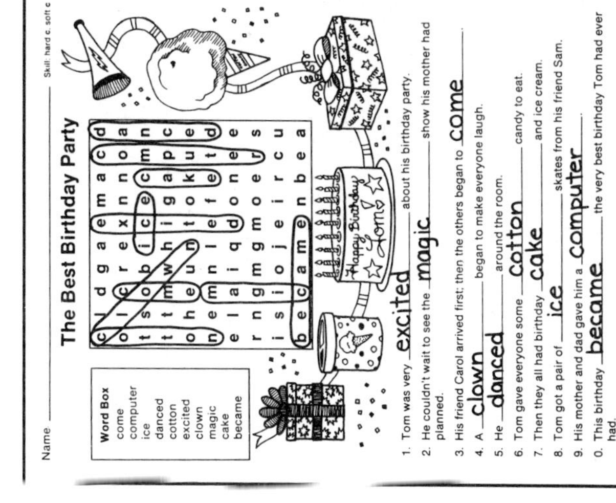

Name ______ Skill: hard c, soft c

The Best Birthday Party

Word Box: come, computer, ice, danced, cotton, excited, clown, magic, cake, became

Happy Birthday Tom

1. Tom was very excited about his birthday party.
2. He couldn't wait to see the magic show his mother had planned.
3. His friend Carol arrived first; then the others began to come.
4. A clown began to make everyone laugh.
5. He danced around the room.
6. Tom gave everyone some cotton candy to eat.
7. Then they all had birthday cake and ice cream.
8. Tom got a pair of ice skates from his friend Sam.
9. His mother and dad gave him a computer.
0. This birthday became the very best birthday Tom had ever had.

Page 98

Answer Key

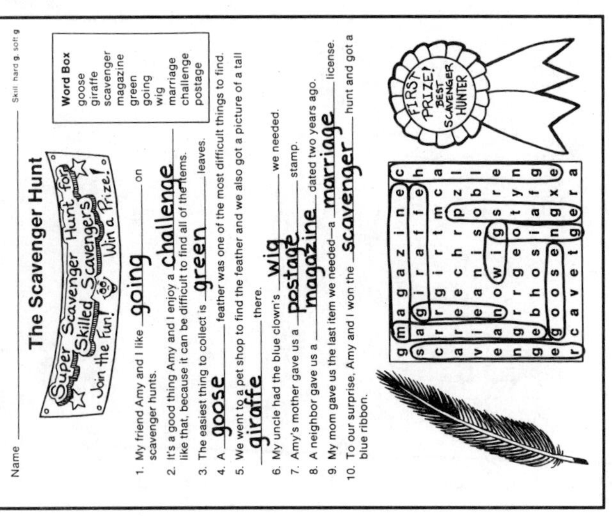

The Scavenger Hunt

Name ______ Skill: hard g, soft g

Super Scavenger Hunt for Skilled Scavengers!
Join the Fun! Win a Prize!

1. My friend Amy and I like going on scavenger hunts.
2. It's a good thing Amy and I enjoy a challenge like that, because it can be difficult to find all of the items.
3. The easiest thing to collect is green leaves.
4. A goose feather was one of the most difficult things to find.
5. We went to a pet shop to find the feather and we also got a picture of a tall giraffe there.
6. My uncle had the blue clown's wig we needed.
7. Amy's mother gave us a postage stamp.
8. A neighbor gave us a magazine dated two years ago.
9. My mom gave us the last item we needed—a marriage license.
10. To our surprise, Amy and I won the scavenger hunt and got a blue ribbon.

Word Box: goose, giraffe, scavenger, magazine, green, going, wig, marriage, challenge, postage

FIRST PRIZE! BEST SCAVENGER HUNTER

Page 99

Name ______ Skill: Phonics, Final y

Read the words in the Word Box.
Write the word that completes each sentence.
Circle the words in the puzzle.

1. Paul asked Dad to read him a story.
2. It is sunny when the sun shines.
3. Mary will try to win the race.
4. Jon was happy to get a new puppy.
5. The new girl in school was very shy.
6. My big brother, Joe, is twenty years old.
7. Why can't we go to the zoo today?
8. The sky is blue today.

Word Box: story, try, shy, why, sunny, happy, sky, twenty

Page 100

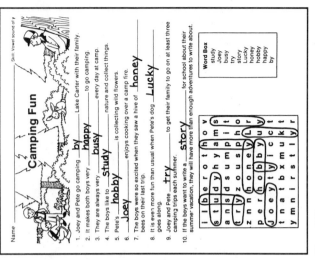

Camping Fun

Name ______ Skill: Vowel sound of y

1. Joey and Pete go camping by Lake Carter with their family.
2. It makes both boys very happy to go camping.
3. They are always very busy every day at camp.
4. The boys like to study nature and collect things.
5. Pete's hobby is collecting wild flowers.
6. Joey enjoys cooking over a camp fire.
7. The boys were so excited when they saw a hive of honey bees on their last trip.
8. It is even more fun than usual when Pete's dog Lucky goes along.
9. Joey and Pete try to get their family to go on at least three camping trips each summer.
10. If the boys want to write a story for school about their summer vacation, they will have more than enough adventures to write about.

Word Box: study, Joey, busy, try, story, Lucky, honey, hobby, happy, by

Page 101

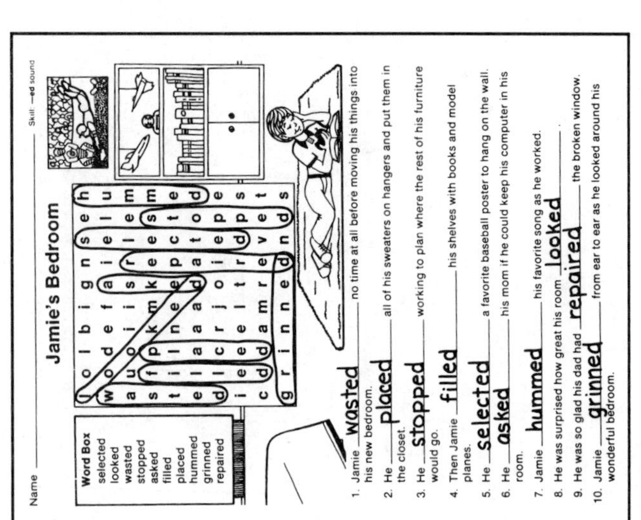

Jamie's Bedroom

Name ______ Skill: -ed sound

Word Box: selected, looked, wasted, stopped, asked, filled, placed, hummed, grinned, repaired

1. Jamie wasted no time at all before moving his things into his new bedroom.
2. He placed all of his sweaters on hangers and put them in the closet.
3. He stopped working to plan where the rest of his furniture would go.
4. Then Jamie filled his shelves with books and model planes.
5. He selected a favorite baseball poster to hang on the wall.
6. He asked his mom if he could keep his computer in his room.
7. Jamie hummed his favorite song as he worked.
8. He was surprised how great his room looked.
9. He was so glad his dad had repaired the broken window.
10. Jamie grinned from ear to ear as he looked around his wonderful bedroom.

Page 102

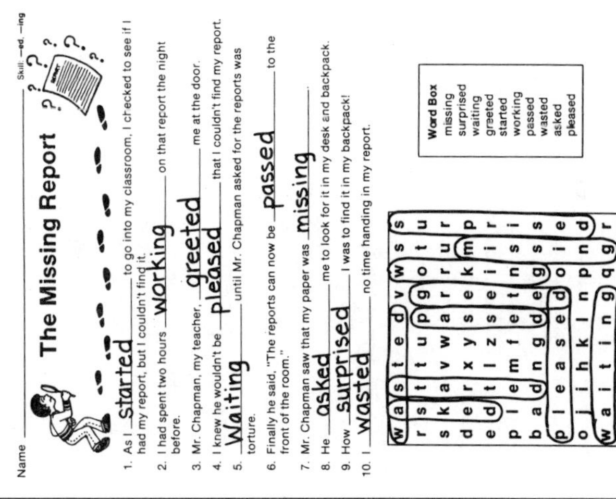

The Missing Report

Name ______ Skill: -ed, -ing

1. As I started to go into my classroom, I checked to see if I had my report, but I couldn't find it.
2. I had spent two hours working on that report the night before.
3. Mr. Chapman, my teacher, greeted me at the door.
4. I knew he wouldn't be pleased that I couldn't find my report.
5. Waiting until Mr. Chapman asked for the reports was torture.
6. Finally he said, "The reports can now be passed to the front of the room."
7. Mr. Chapman saw that my paper was missing.
8. He asked me to look for it in my desk and backpack.
9. How surprised I was to find it in my backpack!
10. I wasted no time handing in my report.

Word Box: missing, surprised, waiting, greeted, started, working, passed, wasted, asked, pleased

Page 103

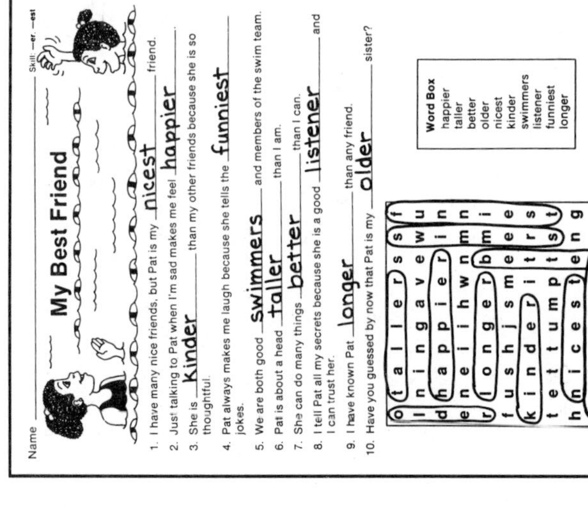

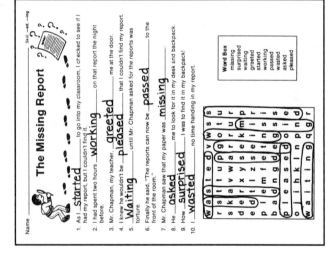

My Best Friend

Name ______ Skill: -er -est

1. I have many nice friends, but Pat is my nicest friend.
2. Just talking to Pat when I'm sad makes me feel happier.
3. She is kinder than my other friends because she is so thoughtful.
4. Pat always makes me laugh because she tells the funniest jokes.
5. We are both good swimmers and members of the swim team.
6. Pat is about a head taller than I am.
7. She can do many things better than I can.
8. I tell Pat all my secrets because she is a good listener and I can trust her.
9. I have known Pat longer than any friend.
10. Have you guessed by now that Pat is my older sister?

Word Box: happier, taller, better, older, nicest, kinder, swimmers, listener, funniest, longer

Page 104